RED LIP
THEOLOGY

RED LIP
THEOLOGY

FOR CHURCH GIRLS WHO'VE CONSIDERED
TITHING TO THE BEAUTY SUPPLY STORE WHEN
SUNDAY MORNING ISN'T ENOUGH

CANDICE MARIE
BENBOW

FOREWORD BY MELISSA HARRIS-PERRY

CONVERGENT

NEW YORK

Published in the United States by Convergent Books, an imprint of
Random House, a division of Penguin Random House LLC, New York.

CONVERGENT BOOKS is a registered trademark and its c colophon
is a trademark of Penguin Random House LLC.

Library of Congress Cataloging-in-Publication Data
Names: Benbow, Candice Marie, author.
Title: Red lip theology / Candice Marie Benbow;
foreword by Melissa Harris-Perry.
Description: First edition. | New York: Convergent, [2022]
Identifiers: LCCN 2021040202 (print) | LCCN 2021040203 (ebook) |
ISBN 9780593238462 (hardcover) | ISBN 9780593238479 (ebook)
Subjects: LCSH: African American women—Religious life. |
Christian women—Religious life.
Classification: LCC BR563.N4 B46 2022 (print) |
LCC BR563.N4 (ebook) | DDC 277.3082089/96073—dc23
LC record available at https://lccn.loc.gov/2021040202
LC ebook record available at https://lccn.loc.gov/2021040203

Printed in Canada

crownpublishing.com

2 4 6 8 9 7 5 3 1

First Edition

Book design by Caroline Cunningham
Title page background image and chapter opening detail: iStock/Sandra M

This book is dedicated to my mother,

Debra Louise Benbow.

You are my north star.

Your love is the scripture that guides my life.

Thank you for introducing me to God and thank you for learning

to give me room to be myself.

May all of my words and every meditation be acceptable to you.

Forever.

FOREWORD

BY MELISSA HARRIS-PERRY

S *in.* It's the name of my favorite red lipstick.

There's no doubt that MAC Cosmetics knew this color, a deep wine with hints of blue undertone, would be beloved by Black women. Which is what makes the name so bothersome. *Sin.* Really? I'm all here for *Naughty, Rowdy,* or even *Trouble,* but it is downright mean to label a Black woman's best red lipstick *Sin.*

Red lipstick is taboo for many girls raised in Black churches or reared in Black families and neighborhoods where religious mores determine collective norms even if the folks enforcing those norms aren't tithing members in good standing of any actual congregation. Shamed for being fast, womanly, or too damn grown, Black girls are encouraged to stop doing so much or being extra.

Red lipstick is definitely extra.

Even when the bank account is empty or emotional resources are low, sisters are taught never to bring raggedy dresses, stockings, shoes, bags, belts, lashes, or nails into the house of the Lord. We're encouraged to adorn our sanctified smiles with a matte lip in taupe, cocoa, or coffee bean. Even a glossy mauve or spice is saintly perfection. But red? Never red. It's printed right there in the name: *Sin*.

Navigating a whole, entire, complicated, cray morality play of righteousness and rouged lips every time you step up to the makeup counter is exhausting. Surely, Black women who shoulder more than our fair share of child-rearing, church-building, community-gathering, bag-securing, and waymaking deserve a God better than some petty, distant patriarch policing our lip color.

Black girls deserve a magnificent, loving, immanent, and chill God. We need a God who loves our minds when we make dean's list and when we peace-out on the PhD. We need a God who loves our hearts even when they are broken as a result of our foreseeably foolish choices. We know God will not shield us from agony when we lose our mama and will not always guard us from the evil of a sexual assault, but we need a God big enough to send our BFFs to our grieving chamber, to gently lure us to the makeup counter, and to help us choose a red lipstick so that we can see ourselves again.

We not only need a God who loves Black girls; we need a God who likes us. Us. Regular Black girls, with nappy hair, big hips, and red lips. Candice Marie Benbow's *Red Lip Theology* is a road map to where we might find the God we need— Winston-Salem, North Carolina.

Listen! I was just as shocked as I imagine you must be to learn this. A somewhat unremarkable city of a quarter million residents nestled in the North Carolina Piedmont,

Winston-Salem is not a beach town or a mountain getaway. It isn't the state's capital or its major metropolitan. The city's tobacco foundations are evident in the twin names that eventually became bestsellers for R. J. Reynolds.

Winston tastes good like a cigarette should!

Lord help us.

Winston-Salem is home of the arguably divine Krispy Kreme doughnuts, but that isn't why Benbow's text uncovers God there. Benbow gets tight with God in Winston-Salem because it is where she finds herself. Benbow was raised in this city I now call home, where I am raising my own daughters. Indeed, my seven-year-old regularly introduces herself as "Anna from Winston-Salem."

I roared with laughter when Benbow journeyed through JCPenney to the "new side" of the mall, shouted with recognition when she recounted Parkland High School football games, and church-lady hummed while giving a judgmental side-eye to the judgmental church folk she describes. Oh, the contradictions!

In short, I see myself in Candice. I feel her. The loving the wrong one. GIRL. The being *over* white folk in the academe. CHILE. The enduring scars of sexual assault. LISTEN. The losing the will to live. PREACH! The clinging to your squad 'cause they are all you got. HALLELUJAH.

Candice from Winston-Salem. It's just an ordinary Blackgirl story. Which means, of course, it isn't ordinary at all.

Poet, playwright, artist, and author Ntozake Shange concludes her magnificent choreopoem *For Colored Girls Who Have Considered Suicide When the Rainbow Is Enuf* by writing:

i found god in myself
and i loved her,
I loved her fiercely.

Adapting Shange, Benbow's subtitle signals that her text is an offering: *For Church Girls Who've Considered Tithing to the Beauty Supply Store When Sunday Morning Isn't Enough.* And like Shange's 1974 play, *Red Lip Theology* discovers the sacred during a pilgrimage through the profane. Benbow's unflinching examination and compassionate appreciation of her own self and soul lead her to the same conclusion as Shange— recognition of the marvelous, messy, red-lip-loving God within.

And because we find ourselves in Benbow, we too find God in ourselves, and love her—fiercely.

Melissa Harris-Perry is the Maya Angelou Presidential Chair in the Department of Politics and International Affairs and the Department of Women, Gender, and Sexuality Studies at Wake Forest University.

CONTENTS

CONTENTS

SUING GOD FOR BACK CHILD SUPPORT

PRIMER

A good primer adds a necessary layer of protection between the healthy skin we've worked hard to nourish and the makeup that will only enhance our beauty. Ensuring the slay can last all day without interruption, it's a reinforcement to preserve what's underneath from whatever is to come.

GOD AND OTHER REFORMED HELICOPTER PARENTS

FOUNDATION

Foundation grounds our look and everything about it. A miscalculation in this step will throw off everything. The wrong foundation can leave us discolored and unable to effectively present our creativity to the world. But the right one? With the right one, everything can come together and we are unstoppable.

GOD MADE ME BLACK

BROWS, EYE SHADOW, LINER, AND LASHES

If eyes are the windows to our souls, then our eye makeup is some really dope blinds and curtains! As we see ourselves, so shall we see the world around us. Reflecting that glory and confidence, through creative eye looks, is its own affirmation.

CONTENTS

AMAZING GRACE FOR SIDE CHICKS

CONTOUR AND CONCEALER

Though we are beautiful, our skin can bear the imperfections left from scrapes, scars, bruises, and stress. Contour and concealer do not hide these imperfections as if they are mistakes or are worthy of shame. Instead, they allow us to incorporate them into the full narrative of our slay.

WE SHOULD ALL BE WOMANISTS

BRONZER

When I said I didn't need to purchase any, a makeup artist once described bronzer to me as the "spirit" of the entire look. It provides the character of the slay. "It shows us who you are," she said. Adding warmth and dimension to our looks, bronzer isn't optional. It's essential.

SURVIVED BY A SPECIAL FRIEND

BLUSH

Blush adds a healthy glow to our skin and a much-needed flush of color to our looks. It is the companion encouraging our smiles to be more truthful and inviting. Blush gives us the confidence to be fierce, free, and honest—all of which remain even after we wash the blush away.

CONTENTS

BLACK LACE TEDDIES AND OTHER PIECES I ROCK UNDER THE ANOINTING

HIGHLIGHTER

Highlighter attracts and reflects light. We cannot hide when we wear it. We are seen in our full glory. And being seen emboldens us to be ourselves in every way imaginable. Because we are enough and we are powerful.

LEAVING CHURCH

LIP PRIMER, LINER, LIP GLOSS, AND LIPSTICK

Our lip products complete the look. And yet, they stand alone and put our mouths on full display. We kiss and speak with boldness. Our lips, decorated and in their power, dare you to look away. And, for us, they call us home.

PSALM 90:12

SETTING SPRAY

Holding everything together, perhaps the setting spray does the most work: taking all of these looks, each stand-alone in its own right, and allowing them to tell one cohesive story. If the look begins to falter, the setting spray is reapplied to reawaken and remind it of its purpose: to slay.

CONTENTS

CONCLUSION

ACKNOWLEDGMENTS

INTRODUCTION

"Candice, I love you." Sheleda said it with all the affection a best friend of twelve years could muster and the concern of the same. "I really want you to start taking better care in how you look. You don't look like my best friend anymore." To be fair, I didn't feel like her either. Sheleda had come to North Carolina for my thirty-first birthday, to lay eyes on me. I'd been struggling and, no matter how much I said I was okay, she knew I wasn't. Fresh off another failed relationship attempt, I'd become defeated and completely let myself go. Sheleda came for the weekend in hopes of reviving me. She and my line sister Tran had a Saturday at the spa and a trip to the mall planned. When I got dressed for the day, I was wearing a pair of faded brown slacks, some overrun navy Mootsies Tootsies loafers, and the white sweater my aunt Darlene gave me for Christmas the year she passed away. Sheleda and Tran were dressed like runway models. *That's* what you're wearing?" Sheleda asked. "She's been looking like this a lot lately," Tran said in response, as if I wasn't there. If I cared, I would've felt a way. It was comfortable and what I wore to teach. "Yeah, but you're not going to teach," Sheleda said. "You're going to the mall. And you shouldn't be wearing that to teach anyway." I rolled my eyes, grabbed the keys, and headed downstairs toward the car. I wasn't changing clothes. The truth is I didn't have anything better to change into anyway.

I didn't have the language for it but I'd been functionally depressed for the better part of 2012. I have never been a skinny girl, but I was gaining a significant amount of weight. There was no energy for doing the things I wanted to do, let alone work out. My hair was a mess. I was a mess. There I was at the mall with my best friend, who was a former beauty queen and model, and my line sister whose line name is Prototype, and I was looking like their great-grandmother. But I couldn't even be one of those. At least their great-grandmothers had been with men long enough to create children and produce the lineages that gave me my homegirls. I couldn't even get a guy to commit to anything beyond being friends or "just kicking it." There was no need to dress up for a trip to the mall. We weren't in high school or college anymore and nobody was checking for me anyway.

I parked at JCPenney, the store connecting the "old" and "new" parts of Hanes Mall in my hometown of Winston-Salem, North Carolina. (I say "old" and "new" as if the "new" part hasn't existed for at least twenty years.) What I thought would be a quick trip to the intimates section—because Mama gave me her Penney's card to get some new bras—and a walk through to the other, more glamorous stores became a life-changing mall excursion. Sheleda and Tran took me to the clothing section and made me pick out an outfit, and I honestly don't know why because they vetoed everything I brought back. Granted, my choices were frumpy and old-looking. But they were comfortable and the lack of style made me feel less embarrassed about the weight I'd gained. Tran and Sheleda took me into the dressing room and came back with several items of clothing until *they* agreed on three outfits for me. We spent ninety dollars. Mama was hot when the statement came a month later and there was no bra in sight.

When we left the clothing section, Sheleda and Tran took me straight to the small Sephora store inside JCPenney to get makeup. I was adamant I didn't want any. "I'm paying for it," Sheleda said. Tran reached in her wallet, gave Sheleda forty dollars, told her to add it to whatever she planned to spend, and instructed me to sit in a chair by the Make Up For Ever display. Then they went to work, as if they were on the clock, matching my skin tone and complexion. At one point, a particular shade Sheleda wanted me to try was empty on the main display so she went into the storage drawer underneath the displays to get it. The sister who actually worked at Sephora was so offended, I couldn't help but laugh.

I left the Sephora inside of JCPenney with foundation from Make Up For Ever, the Urban Decay Naked eye shadow palette, and Sephora's lipstick in the shade Crush. It was the perfect berry color and would be my all-time favorite until they discontinued it. Reeling from sticker shock, I convinced Sheleda and Tran I would buy concealer, blush, and brushes from

Walmart. While the stuff we tried on in Sephora was amazing, there was no need to spend an exorbitant amount of money on something I wasn't going to wear.

But, before she went back home to Illinois, Sheleda made me promise to wear it. She asked me to make my face every day and put more emphasis into my appearance. She told me it was time to get back to myself. And Sheleda held me as I broke down and told her I didn't know how to find my way back. Besides academic degrees, I didn't have anything to show for my life. What was I even getting back to?

As only best friends can do, Sheleda assured me my life mattered and had purpose beyond what I'd diminished it to because I couldn't see it. And she reminded me the wedding we'd been meticulously planning since we met each other was going to happen. Then she pulled out the card from Tiffany & Co. with information for my dream ring on it. Sheleda told me she'd carried it around in her wallet waiting to pass it along to the right guy one day. I promised my best friend, the greatest person I knew next to my mother, that I would try.

And I did.

I made my face daily. I began working out again and built my wardrobe back to something resembling what a woman in her early thirties would wear. And I bought new shoes; I had no choice. Sheleda watched me throw away the Mootsies Tootsies before she left. I don't think I've experienced genuine comfort in a shoe since. Daily, while attending Duke and teaching sociology at Campbell University, I made intentional efforts to honor the promise I made to Leda. And when I found myself running out of product, I went to the Ulta and

Sephora stores right down the street to restock. Each time, I tried a new product and ventured into more color. When I paid over twenty dollars for Too Faced's Better Than Sex mascara when it launched, I knew I'd lost my mind. Who in the world pays twenty dollars for mascara? But I saw it as a long overdue investment. I was piecing myself together and vowed I wouldn't get that low again. Alongside my commitment to honoring my best friend's wishes for me and attending seminary, something else was happening. I was being radicalized. The old me was being disrupted and a new me was emerging.

That same year, 2012, two events—the death of Whitney Houston and the Black Church's response to the killing of Rekia Boyd—would forever revolutionize how I understood religion's role in the oppression of Black women and my religious institution's complicity in it. Whitney's death rocked me to the core. While I'd never met her, I felt like I knew her. To me, she was the ultimate church girl. Publicly, she embodied everything we're told we should be: beautiful, chaste, and poised. Privately, she wrestled with the demons that come along with trying desperately to live up to those false standards of holiness and purity. When her private struggles became public, church folk turned their backs away and noses up in disgust. They love to say, "I'm praying for you," and "We will be here to help you get well," in one breath. And in the next, they're telling anybody who will listen what you did, when you did it, how you knew better and ought to be ashamed of yourself.

When Whitney died, I lost faith in the possibility we could outgrow the church's hold. The realist in me slowly began to concede, if we didn't prematurely die, we'd spend the rest of our lives trying to unlearn and outrun what the church did to us. It felt too late for me—I'd spent my formative years in the church and the damage had already been done. But it wasn't too late for the generations of Black girls who were coming behind me. They deserve a faith free from the pressure of a perfection impossible to obtain. Whitney died February 11, 2012. The day after her funeral, I drafted my personal essay for my MDiv application for admission the upcoming fall.

On Sunday, March 25, 2012, Black male pastors across the country stood behind the sacred desk to preach the word of God while wearing hoodies. In solidarity, "Hoodie Sunday" was a Black Christian response to the murder of seventeen-year-old Trayvon Martin the month before. For many younger millennials and members of Generation Z, Trayvon's death was the wake-up call and entrance into activism. The Sanford, Florida, Police Department's hesitance to arrest Trayvon's killer made it clear not much had changed. It was in such a charged and emotional moment that Alicia Garza, Patrisse Cullors, and Opal Tometi coined the statement and hashtag "Black Lives Matter," which later became a global movement for change.

These pastors scheduled several conference calls in the weeks leading up to "Hoodie Sunday" to ensure everyone was on board with the messaging. It was important congregations across the country understood what happened to Trayvon and how the police's refusal to relentlessly pursue justice left our young Black boys vulnerable. "Hoodie Sunday" was one of the most powerful Black Church moments in modern history. When it came to fighting for justice and equal protection under the law, the service showed the Black Church had not lost its way.

Yet, on March 21, 2012—just a few days before "Hoodie Sunday"—Rekia Boyd was murdered by an off-duty police officer in Chicago and no intention was made to speak her name alongside Trayvon's at the coordinated services. In fact, many pastors did not mention her at all. When pressed about this on social media, some pastors deflected and claimed they mentioned her in their sermons or were leaving it up to their respective youth and women's ministries to honor her.

The omission of Rekia from any institutionalized moment reinforced Black churches' refusal to see the conditions and experiences of Black girls and women as the same as those of Black boys and men. I watched the murders of Black boys and men command national, even global, attention while the deaths of Black girls and women were dismissed as unfortunate, but avoidable. "Hoodie Sunday" and the Black Church's collective silence about Rekia and insert-the-name-of-any-other-Black-girl-or-woman-who-has-been-a-victim-of-state-or-intimate-partner-or-sexual-violence-here drove home the point I, and other sisters, should never forget: if we are killed, the church won't even care.

With the loss and mistreatment of Whitney and Rekia as the backdrop of the first year of my MDiv program, I selected classes which pushed me to engage scripture much more critically. Consequently, the work in those courses challenged my thinking about who I was and the faith I wanted for myself. I'd spent so much time battling what I didn't know was depression, the shame of failed relationships and singleness, because I labored under the belief that experiencing both made me less of a woman—more specifically, less of a godly woman. I should have been married and on baby number two. Having no man or child in sight obviously meant something was wrong with me.

So much of Western Christianity is rooted in the subjugation of women, and I had been reared in a faith tradition which largely existed to give Black men the status and power White people refused them in larger society. On a much broader scale, the rights of women were nonexistent because God said so and, within my context, Black women couldn't get free until Black men did. For centuries, Black and White women bemoaned these beliefs but not much change came as a result. There have been strides but no true paradigm shift. That's how my unmarried mother could still be expected to stand—by herself—and apologize to the congregation for being pregnant with me. It's how Black men could go—or not go—to divinity school and rise to power by preaching to Black women about what we need to do to become better, godly women who get chosen by "good" Black men.

Sitting in those divinity school classes, doing the work of piecing myself back together, honoring the promise I'd made to Sheleda, and coming to terms with my own radicalization did something to me. First, it pissed me off. I found myself constantly angry at the fact men upheld and benefited from systems they knew were harming women at the core of our humanity. My anger made me look for more truth. It was in divinity school when I fully engaged womanist theology, which is an entire theological discourse grounded in Black women's relationship with God and how our relationship with the Divine impacts and is impacted by the world around us. I had been introduced to this perspective in undergrad, but I didn't really "get" it. I appreciated the ways it called out sexism in the church. But there was so much more to it than that.

Reading books like Jacquelyn Grant's *White Women's Christ and Black Women's Jesus* pushed me to recognize the fundamentally different person Black and White women are talking about when they discuss their savior. Even still, I didn't realize how much womanist theology could and would reorient my theological perspective. It gave me the language to walk toward understanding Black women and God more, both separately and as a collective, but it didn't go far enough. Yet even as I desired to navigate it, womanist theology didn't feel like it was created for women like me: sisters who didn't tuck in their ratchetness in favor of righteousness to occupy certain spaces or get in certain rooms. I needed something to speak to the totality of who I am. From that desire and a snarky conversation with a clueless White boy, red lip theology was born.

Part of the Duke Divinity School academic paradigm requires a Black Church Studies course for graduation, and I hadn't met but a handful of White students who enjoyed it. In those classes, White Christians were introduced to Black theologians and elements of the Black religious experience. Class after class, I watched them struggle to reconcile how Black people understood and articulated God outside of their purview, and because they couldn't understand it, they deemed it demonic or infantile. In a course on the works of the great theologian and mystic Howard Thurman, a White male classmate said Thurman needed to be "disciplined" against the early church fathers and other theologians to see if his work had validity and merit. Tensions in the class were high. Our professor, also dean of Duke Chapel, Luke Powery, had to take the bulk of one class session to address the bubbling tension, and I took that as a sign from the heavens to tell each and every White classmate what I thought about them, their covert racism, and where they could stick their theologians who were capable of disciplining. It made for an interesting remainder of the semester.

When Black folk called them out on their racism at Duke, our White classmates loved to follow up with invitations for coffee and lunch to assure us they weren't racist. After I told my classmates Thurman didn't need to be disciplined but they needed Jesus, I lost count of how many wanted me to meet them in the divinity school's refectory so I could hear their hearts. I declined every offer. One classmate was insistent, though, and sat at the table with me in the library. Now, if I would've gotten up and left—like I wanted to do—I knew it would've been obvious why I did. And I was actually trying to be more like Jesus that day. So I stayed.

"So, Candice, let me ask you something," he started. I mustered a fake smile to feign interest in what I knew was about to be foolishness. "Do you consider yourself a Black theologian or are you a regular theologian?"

For a moment, I stared at this White dude, who was from either Texas or the Midwest (because the most incredulous ones came from there). Who was either Baptist or Methodist (because the most insufferable ones were). I stared at him, contemplating how I would start the read. Would I go for the obvious and ask him how dare he insult the entire Black religious tradition by suggesting it was somehow abnormal? Or would I be a bit more subtle, asking him about last week's readings—knowing he hadn't done them—and then say he didn't even have the range to know what theology is in the first place?

While I found joy in each option, I was also tired of trying to push classmates like him to recognize the value in our theologies and biblical interpretations. Nothing I said was going to convince him of anything, so why would I even try? "I'm . . . I'm a red lip theologian." Before I even realized I said it, it was out there. But it felt right.

"What is that? Who started that?" My classmate seemed intrigued and slightly embarrassed. I don't know if he was actually interested in what I was saying or afraid he'd missed red lip theology in one of our readings.

Either way, I was done with the conversation. "I did. Just now," I said as I packed up my things and left.

Something amazing happened after I told my classmate I was a red lip theologian. I began to feel more confident in my ability to articulate my faith and what it meant for me. But, as good as it felt, I had to ask myself a very important question. What is red lip theology?

Red lip theology is the lens through which I understand myself as a millennial Black woman of faith. It creates space for both my upbringing in the Black Baptist Church of the

South and my coming of age when America was embracing hip-hop's aggressive, brash voice and bringing it into the mainstream. Red lip theology is the space in which young, Black churchwomen can sit with the parts of ourselves and be honest about all of them. Within these borders, there are boundless possibilities for who we can become and how we can live into our faith. Red lip theology introduced me to a God much more kind, gracious, and loving than the one I'd been given in my youth and young adulthood. And all of this was a result of keeping a promise to my best friend while being transformed by the renewing of my mind. Red lip theology gave God back to me, me back to God, and me back to myself.

That sounds beautiful and revolutionary, doesn't it? Don't get me wrong. Parts of it were. But I wasn't fully prepared for what embracing red lip theology would bring up in me. I had no choice but to confront what I believed and why I believed it. I was in a rigorous academic program, and, for me, it was impossible to resist the powerful scope of theological study. I say "for me" because I know people who have the same degree I have and advanced degrees in theology and biblical study who are just as bigoted and closed-minded as they were before they entered their programs. Transformation is a choice. Some aspects of what I believed growing up just didn't serve me anymore. Maybe they never served me and I didn't realize it. Maybe that's why I took Whitney's death and the dismissal of Rekia so hard. There was something within me that knew better was possible.

When I began to challenge religious presuppositions, I

learned Black Christians could be as violent as racist White folks. Online, they became trolls—harassing me with scriptures and links to two- and three-hour-long YouTube videos detailing how wrong I was and damning me to Hell. And, when I got too specific about which pastors were engaging in dangerous rhetoric, that's when "touch not my anointed" turned into threats of bodily harm and sexual assault. It escapes me the number of times a man has threatened to come put something in my mouth when I dared to discuss how the Black Church has been violent toward Black women. People, including friends and loved ones, distanced themselves from me. According to them, I was drifting away. I'd gotten too smart and was intellectualizing myself out of God and the faith. In my adulthood, my fiercest arguments with my mother were about the ways my feminism and faith were merging together. What she and others couldn't see was that red lip theology brought me closer to God than I'd ever been in my life.

And I would need that closeness when Mama unexpectedly died six months after my graduation from Duke and two months before she was scheduled to defend her dissertation. I would need to feel God close to me when the man I'd started having an affair with during my first year of seminary divorced his wife and immediately married someone else. I would need every angel encamped around me when a date ended in sexual assault. I would need the compassionate God who is also serious about justice and equity when pursuing a PhD at one of the top theological institutions in the world brought me face-to-face with the evils of evangelical racism. I would need my ancestors and the orishas when all of this came to a head and I ended up in the hospital for suicidal ideation and major depression just days after preaching a Good Friday sermon. I would need that closeness to God when I summoned every ounce of strength I did and did not have to piece my life back together, embrace the beauty of it, and fully live into its glory.

There are many things red lip theology is not. This isn't prescriptive for all women. I say "all women" because, while I'm clear I'm talking to and about Black women from my perspective as one, other women are eavesdropping and looking for freedom, too. I like to call that "overflow." It's not prescriptive because I hate when people, especially Black preaching men, try to make their preaching and analysis apply to everyone when it doesn't. There's no one-size-fits-all solution to life and the people who say, "yes, there is—it's Jesus" are being lazy and willfully obtuse.

While I want all Black women of faith to recognize and denounce the patriarchal and sexist foundations of religion and institutional church spaces the same way I do, I know that's not realistic. Some sisters recoil at the sight of feminist movements intersecting with faith. Others are deeply rooted and afraid to pluck up some things. A few have even been offended by pretty much everything I say and have no problems telling me as much. A group of church girl bullies even made a YouTube video "refuting" me. I don't know who has time to sit around for three hours to talk about someone they don't like "for the sake of the gospel" but, apparently, they did. I'm not centering any of them with this work either. While I'm here for all Black women, I'm clear I'm not here for every sister. I'm talking to women like me who long for something more—who believe the goodness and the love of God aren't reserved for a select group but are for all who inhale and exhale. I am talking to the sisters who desire their faith and feminism to fit together without force.

I am many things. I'm a daughter. I am an only child who also has two half brothers. I am a Southern girl, and even though I could stand to lose a few pounds, I am pretty vain about my shape. I'm smart and try to stay up on current events. I set out to read twelve new books a year, though I barely get through eight or nine. I try to do right by my family, especially my grandmother and my cousins Mark and Reggie. I consider myself to be a good friend, and I really try to be a good person.

I'm a hot mess, too.

I'm spoiled and typically don't understand why things can't just be the way I said they needed to be. My slick mouth has always gotten me into trouble, and I can use this beautiful gift of words I have to cut folks deep. I have said and done some cringeworthy things. At times, I have disappointed people who loved and saw the best in me, and I've disappointed myself. But, no matter what condition I find myself in at any given moment, I know I am fully loved by God.

My faith is grounded in the teachings of Jesus, the wisdom of the ancestors, and the power of Black womanhood. Each has saved my life over and over again. While my faith doesn't look like what it used to, I am learning to give myself an abundance of grace and push beyond the limits of my past and my pain. I don't know what all I will be in this life but I know I can be whole and free.

Red Lip Theology represents the journey. It details how I went from the haggard in Mootsies Tootsies and slacks to the "bad bish" who can't stay out of bodycons and bright pumps. It's about how the relationship between my bible and my Sephora Beauty Insider card changed my life. It is the story of a freedom, hard fought and even harder won. In this space, the bruises are real but colorful rouges of blush remind me I am always more than what hurt me. Here, contour and concealer hide what doesn't need to be seen at a given moment but cede to "Skin Care Saturday" rituals and give me the freedom to stand in the fullness of who I am, flaws and all.

Here I share how a life, even with its valleys and deserts, can still be lush and bountiful when it's guided by love, grace, and truth. Patterned after the necessary steps for achieving a flawless face, these essays fully embody what these beauty practices uncovered for me and frame what I hope will be a progressive faith dialogue for millennial Black women.

My skin-care and makeup routines are pretty sacred to me. Everything stops in the morning and evening when I'm taking care of my skin. Each morning, I take myself through a ten-step skin-care regimen (oil cleanser, cream cleanser, exfoliant, toner, essence, ampoule, serum, sheet masks, eye cream, moisturizer with SPF sunscreen) while listening to Juanita Bynum's *Morning Glory* album. In the evening, those same steps are set to Stevie Wonder's *Journey Through the Secret Life of Plants*. (I've been obsessed since my godbrother Dustin introduced me to it in 2018.)

And it doesn't matter where I'm going, whenever I'm applying makeup, I'm listening to *Anti* by Rihanna. I could be getting ready for church; I'll just be listening to "Yeah, I Said It" while preparing to go hear the word. RiRi released *Anti* at a time when nothing in my life was going right and makeup therapy was one of the few things holding me together. The album provided escape and refuge; it still does.

When I told her this, my friend Shayla encouraged me to turn my makeup application into its own ritual, too. She suggested I name my brushes and speak affirmations over myself. With Rihanna in the background, I ask God and my ancestors to keep me grounded in what I know to be true as I apply my foundation. I remind myself that the visions and dreams for my life will come to fruition as I play with those colorful eye shadow palettes I love so much. As I smile and apply blush, I tell myself I am confident and full of wonder. And, as I'm choosing from the over two hundred lipsticks I own to just wear one of the same ten, I set the intention that everything I speak will bring life to me, those I love, and the world around me. These remain among the most sacred parts of my day.

I invite you into this space with me, where we can learn and grow together. It's a space where we can look back on the past, wince a bit—and laugh too—but see how it unfolds into the wondrous future before us. You may not have a Sheleda who will gather you in your own "Mootsies Tootsies" moment. Or you may have her but are afraid to tell her the truth. Either way, I hope this book offers the permission you need to get it together and get free. That's my deepest prayer as you travel through these pages.

Creating an authentic faith rooted in a love for God, creation, and oneself is not easy work. It is a lifelong journey. I am in it for the long haul but I need more travel buddies. If you're ready, slide into those heels or lace up your sneakers, grab your MAC Ruby Woo, Cruella by NARS, or the Lip Bar's Bawse Lady and let's go!

RED LIP
THEOLOGY

WE ARE GOOD CREATION

As far as childhoods go, I had an amazing one. Surrounded by books I read under covers well past my bedtime and Barbie dolls whose feet I chewed and hair I cut into asymmetrical bobs. I took ballet, tap, and jazz at one of Winston-Salem's premier dance studios with rich White girls and middle-class Black ones like me. I had piano lessons after my private school recessed for the day; I was in Girl Scouts from the time I was in kindergarten till I graduated high school with my Gold Award; and I had every enrichment program in between. I had the best of everything and was given opportunities to excel in life. Despite this, though, I could not escape one fatal flaw: my mother wasn't married to my father.

Even as a child, I understood my mother's singleness as her fault. That's how family and church folk made it seem. Somehow, she'd gotten pregnant and had a baby by herself. Committed to ensuring I understood my responsibility to my community and to Black people, Mama took me to town hall meetings, public forums, and any other place where the state of Black America was discussed. There, I heard reports of how single motherhood gutted our community of its morals and standards. Daniel Patrick Moynihan released his "take" on the fate of Black America in 1965—summarized by the line, "In essence, the Negro community has been forced into a matri- archal structure which, because it is too out of line with the rest of the American society, seriously retards the progress of the group as a whole, and imposes a crushing burden on the Negro male and, in consequence, on a great many Negro women as well." * And, though the report was met with great resistance and critique, many Black folks shared his senti- ments. In those town hall meetings, some were extremely vocal in their belief that the problem with Black America was Black women and had no qualms about saying that when given a microphone. Others refused to deny the crushing weight of inequality and how our communities suffered be- cause of it, while at the same time subtly suggesting that we as Black people could do more to stop imposing added suf- fering onto our lives.

Black men *couldn't* be fathers for a number of reasons, they told us. Many were dead or incarcerated thanks to the drug trade and subsequent war on it. Others were unable to come to terms with the limitations America imposed on Black men and, consequently, couldn't be adequate and present fathers. The least single Black mothers could do was pick up the

* Daniel Patrick Moynihan. *The Negro Family: The Case for National Action* (commonly known as the Moynihan Report). U.S. Department of Labor (United States: Cosimo, 2019).

slack, keep their kids well groomed, adequately fed, off the streets and out of trouble for the sake of communal uplift. Taking responsibility wasn't too much to ask and doing so was their reasonable service, the penance they paid to God for being disobedient and getting knocked up in the first place.

Mama made sure I grew up in church. She told me she took the promise Hannah made to God in 1 Samuel seriously. If God got her and her child out of the despair of her circumstances, she'd give me back to God. As a single mother raising a Black girl during the height of the crack epidemic and the rise of gang violence, Mama believed the church would keep me safe. And with a teen growing up while hip-hop was still finding its way, she also believed the church would keep me chaste. The church was the solution for single, Christian Black women raising Black girls, as it had been the solution for so many Black women before them.

Black people have always been a spiritual people, but nobody is more spiritual than Black women. To love God and the Spirit is the legacy of Black women. But while mothers of millennial Black girls were sending their daughters to church to escape the perils of the world, we also became victims of the traps set in the holiest of places. It was in church where I learned, as a child, I had the butt and breasts of a grown woman. Too many of us were preyed upon in the places where our mothers thought we were safe. And we couldn't tell them because we didn't want them to feel the guilt of being unable to keep us protected.

Single motherhood is a stain, the scarlet letter in our community. Even the bright lights of my childhood couldn't blind me to the reality that my mother wasn't supposed to do this alone. And, on any given Sunday, we'd hear about it. I remember the sermons where pastors told single women to keep their legs closed so they wouldn't find themselves in whatever mess they were in. It was actually in church where I learned what it meant to be born "out of wedlock." One of my Sunday School teachers used me as an example to teach the concept. Decades later, Mama told me my teacher did that in retaliation for my mother being named to the pastoral search committee. In no uncertain terms, it was reinforced that, if my mother truly loved God and obeyed His word, I wouldn't even be here.

Yet, the community and the church weren't the only places my mother endured the stigma of being pregnant and unmarried. Mama shared with me the scorn of and remarks made by family members when she became pregnant. Though she wasn't the first person in our family to occupy unwed mother status, she was the first to graduate college and was heavily involved in church. She was doing the right things and, according to relatives who resented it, she felt like she was better than everybody else. And though she wasn't a teen mother like others in our family and had a successful career and her own apartment, my mother's pregnancy was seen as proof she wasn't as perfect as people said she purported to be. Other women in my family got pregnant and married their children's fathers (or someone willing to claim them, as I would learn years later) either before or shortly after delivery. By the time I came along, these families were well established and their children's origins well concealed and long forgotten. That wasn't the case for my mother. She and my father never married and she didn't marry anyone else. She raised her shame by herself.

Raising a Black girl alone in the eighties and nineties couldn't have been easy. My mother made it look like it was, though. She did her level best to instill a pride in me for being alive. When I was old enough to understand it, my mother shared with me the greatest step she'd taken to prove she knew being pregnant with me wasn't wrong. In her church and many churches at the time, unmarried pregnant women were expected to come before the church, confess their sin, and ask for the church to forgive them. Very rarely, if ever, were the expectant fathers made to do the same thing. When the time came for my mother to apologize for being pregnant with me, she couldn't do it. She told me, no matter what happened between her and my father, she couldn't stand in front of people and call me a mistake. I wasn't sin.

She had understood the repercussions of her defiant jubilation, though things at church and at home became difficult for her to navigate. Feeling the weight of it, my mother attended an evening service at Mercy Seat Holy Church, another small congregation in our hometown. She told me how the isolation forced her to pray for a miracle—my father getting his act together so we could be a family. She knew that was about as possible as snow in the summertime, but it was what she wanted. It would quiet the critics and give her baby the life she deserved to have. And yet, God had other plans. During a sermon about God's provision and protection existing beyond our understanding, Mama said she felt me kick inside of her for the first time. She took the moment as a sign of many things, including the need to truly abandon any hopes she had of a reconciliation with my father. More than anything, she understood such a sacred moment as God making it clear she and her daughter would be okay. As long as they were together and remained close to God, there would be no obstacle they couldn't overcome.

I don't know how long it took my mother to finally end things with my father. She loved him and had a child with him. Walking away from the man you loved and the father of your child would present its own challenges. Yet, I know it didn't take long for her to fully embrace her pregnancy as perfectly aligned with God's will for her life. She'd often say to me, "You've got something amazing to do at a certain time in your life and God had to get you here however he could so you could do it when the time comes." Even though I knew she truly believed I had this enormous life's purpose, sometimes I felt like Mama just said that to me because she knew I didn't believe it.

Mama did all she could to ensure I wouldn't feel the tangible effects of my father's absence. Years before she passed, she confessed the glamorous childhood I had, filled with vacations every summer and annual winter recitals, was her way of making sure I didn't lack because my father didn't want to be there. Even at great sacrifice to her own dreams and well-being, Mama wanted to prove, through my adjustment and exposure, the detractors wrong. In our family and church, there were running bets I'd go off to college, become "buck wild," get pregnant, and be forced to drop out. It would be years before I could see the projection behind their doubts about me, because others had insecurities about their own lives and unmet goals. But, as a child, I didn't understand how people could be so mean. It made no sense that people would see a Black woman raising her daughter to thrive, and root for them both to fail. Mama tried her best to ensure those negative words and energies didn't seep into my spirit. One of my greatest prayers throughout my life was, when she learned they did, she didn't internalize it as her fault.

The truth is, while I spent my childhood enjoying it, I didn't believe I deserved it. I never felt good enough. No matter how much my mother loved me, what could I really be worth if my father didn't? Maybe those people at church and those family members were right. Maybe I didn't belong here. And so I did everything to prove I did. Getting A's and B's in school came easy. I'd figured if my grades were good enough, they would prove Mama could raise an accomplished child on her own. Ironically, my desire to excel in school never translated into getting good grades in conduct. For every A and B on my report card, there were also an N (Needs Improvement) and a U (Unsatisfactory) for excessive talking and disruption. And what kind of child was I if, despite the sacrifices Mama was making for me at home, I couldn't keep my mouth shut at school? Other kids could do it. Why couldn't I? There were girls in my elementary school—girls like Sherwana Hart—who were sweet, kind, smart students. Sherwana got good grades and was quiet in class. She was the kind of daughter my mother deserved. Why couldn't I be more like Sherwana?

I internalized everything about me as unworthy. At first, I thought it was my size and appearance. If I wasn't so fat and ugly, then people would think my mother was doing a good job as a single mom, they would ease up on talking about her and me, and everything would be okay. There was one problem, though. Food became my solace and, as a child, I used emotional eating as a crutch. I was in the sixth grade and a student at Cedar Forest Christian School when one of the White girls told me about bingeing and purging. For about a week, I ate and went straight to the bathroom. That behavior was short-lived when Mama caught me trying to make myself throw up. And I was glad she found me; purging wasn't going to be my thing. But food remained my way of escape, my way of grappling with the desire for people to like me, the desire to be worthy of my mother, the frustration of feeling like neither was attainable.

Perhaps this is the greatest truth I can tell: I never felt worthy of Mama. She was God to me. Mama's womb was the first home I knew and she would always be my most perfect sanctuary. But I felt like I'd ruined her. The first in our family to graduate from college, Mama was following in her mother's footsteps and pursuing her career as a nurse. Then I came along—destroying the legacy she was creating. She was leading our family into uncharted territory, and it was my fault she would continue the "generational curse" of unwed mothers in our family and community. She was on track to be among those who defied the stereotypes, but I put a stop to that. There is no telling who my mother could have been or what she would have done if she'd not become pregnant with me. When we'd run into her teachers from high school and college, they'd make a point to tell me how smart Mama was.

She was one of the brightest students in her class and the teachers had high hopes for her. And Mama had high hopes for herself. She'd start and stop her graduate program twice while I was growing up, and waited until I went off to college to begin again. Although she said she had no regrets and believed her dreams needed to take a back seat to ensure I was able to experience what childhood had to offer—I had the regrets. When we buried her two months before she was set to defend her dissertation, I couldn't help but think she would have had her PhD already if she hadn't had me.

But Mama wanted to have me. She wanted *me*. She wanted to be my mother and spent my entire childhood dismantling church doctrines suggesting I was insufficient because she wasn't married. I'd come to expect that whenever we'd leave church after hearing a sermon shaming single mothers and their children, we'd have a certain conversation on the way home. I almost knew it by heart. "Don't listen to them, Candice. Half of that wasn't nowhere in the bible. God gave you to me and me to you. You understand?" When my "Yes, ma'am" from the back seat was too muffled for her to hear, she'd tell me to look at her when she was talking to me, and our eyes would meet in the rearview mirror of our red Ford Festiva. After a family gathering when she'd overhear something mean said to me or I'd confess to her what was said, she'd tell me that particular family member's fatal flaw. "Now, what room do they have to say anything about you and how you got here?" Then, she'd flash the smile that let me know everything would be all right and told me not to repeat what she just said lest I get into trouble. I knew what my mama was doing. She was working overtime to combat the messages I heard in the very places she'd thought I'd be safe. But the safest place I would ever be was always with her.

There was something about the insistence in Psalm 51:5—how we are born in sin and shaped in iniquity—that renewed shame in me whenever I heard it. It just felt mean. And, for me growing up, it seemed only to be true of children like me. At least that's how folks made me feel. Yet these same people, who couldn't wait to tell me I was a bastard baby and throw it in my mother's face that she was an unwed mother, were the folks who would shout all over the church about being a wretch undone who God decided to redeem one day. Even to a child, it seemed nonsensical. How are you going to judge somebody for being a sinner while you openly admit you used to be a sinner, too?

And when it came to Mama, that's what truly angered me. It wasn't like she was sleeping around and there were men coming in and out of our apartment, because neither of those things was true. These people weren't judging my mama on something she was actively doing; they were judging her on something she'd done in her past. It didn't make sense. We rarely missed church on Sunday and attended bible study every Wednesday. Mama was gainfully employed, active in her community and local alumni association, and voted in every election. What was the problem? Though she was a model citizen, Mama lived in open rebellion against God and the church. To them, it didn't matter how good she was. She was a single mother who refused to apologize for it and refused to cultivate shame in her daughter. She moved through the world and raised me as if she didn't have anything to hang her head about, and that pissed people off. She was accomplished and pushing me to be the same. But no matter how much we'd achieve, her single motherhood would be the trump card some used against her morality, and I felt like it was my fault.

I grew up in faith communities where inferiority and insufficiency became calling cards of God's grace. You knew how much God loved you based on how bad off you were when God found you. Folks would get up and testify about how they used to be liars, cheaters, abusers, drunks—all-around terrible people before God saved them. Essentially, such a dichotomy is our faith story. We are people who don't deserve to live but God pitied us enough to spare our lives. We embrace it and wear those testimonies as if they are badges of honor. And I'm not saying there's something wrong with being happy Jesus saves; that's the crux of our faith. What is troubling is how much we disparage ourselves apart from Jesus's salvation. When we talk about who we were prior to our encounter with Jesus, it's not from a place of affirmation or abundance. And it makes sense, I guess. If you were "good," why would you need God? Yet, there is so much at stake when we buy into the notion we are totally depraved creatures in need of a redemptive savior.

While Mama had already introduced me to Black feminist writers like bell hooks, Angela Davis, Toni Morrison, and Zora Neale Hurston, it wasn't until I went off to Tennessee State University that I was really able to study them. I took a class, The Black Woman, in the Africana Studies Department and spent the entire semester breaking down how social and structural systems work overtime to suppress Black women. It was in this class that I first learned of womanist theology. I didn't spend much time with it then, but I saw how scholars like Evelyn Higginbotham and Cheryl Townsend Gilkes laid bare the way religious ideologies concerning our bodies function as tools of regulation. The class also provided my first encounter with the term "cult of true womanhood," a nineteenth-century concept which upheld the ideals to be valued by women. According to the concept, "true women" were to be pious, chaste, and submissive. In every way possible, they were to embody the biblical standard of womanhood found in Proverbs 31 and Ephesians 5 and 6. And while they were unrealistic for several reasons, it was also problematic how these ideals excluded Black women. Because Black women were brought to the Americas as chattel slaves, White people didn't see them as "women"; they didn't even see them as human.

In her book *Righteous Discontent: The Women's Movement in the Black Baptist Church, 1880–1920*, Higginbotham details how Black churchwomen would employ the "politics of respectability" as a means of entering the cult of true womanhood by proxy, thus being seen as Black women worthy of respect. Today, "respectability politics" is often shorthand for ways Black people attempt to cater to Whiteness, but it means so much more. The politics of respectability was a method of survival in a world where Black women couldn't find safety anywhere. For Black Christians, though, respectability did become a way of life, a measuring stick used to prove how righteous one truly was. As a college sophomore, I began to recognize the relationship between the ways our religious communities would both embrace theologies positioning us as wretched and completely embrace respectability politics. And it was very much connected to how White people still saw and treated us. If we realized we needed God and lived according to who God called us to be, then we would be holy and our people would be holy. And our people wouldn't be in society's last place. No matter how much our churches loved Dr. King and the Civil Rights Movement, no matter how much they talked about injustice, it was becoming clearer to me that a fundamental tenet of being a Black Christian was believing Black people were the problem.

Consequently, I began to wrestle with the idea of my inferiority. Because if I believed it—if I believed there was something wrong with me because my mother wasn't married—I would do whatever I could to ensure I didn't do the same thing. I would make sure I wasn't like my mama. And that didn't sit well with me. The beauty of college, to me, was the beauty of my twenties: I was reading everything, absorbing knowledge like a sponge. Of course that meant I knew absolutely everything. I came home and declared to my mother the Black Church was a sexist organization that hated Black women. She told me the Black Church could be whatever I needed it to be in Nashville but, when I came home on breaks, I better be in church Sunday morning.

The complication of my twenties was I didn't really know how to articulate my disagreement just yet, and I didn't really know *why* I didn't believe in the church as a worthwhile project anymore. More important, I didn't know if I could believe certain things about feminism and sexuality and still remain a Christian. Truth be told, unlearning might be a lifelong effort.

At Duke Divinity—eight years after my Africana Studies class at TSU—creation care was a pretty big deal. There were courses on it, symposiums were held to discuss it, and food sourcing and preparation by the campus refectory were guided by ethical principles grounded in it. One of the discipline's foremost scholars, Norman Wirzba, taught there and graciously engaged in these conversations whenever we approached him. As a theological discourse, creation care is just what its name suggests. It's the idea we should actually care about creation. God took such great time and intention to bring creation into being; humanity should do more to honor and protect it. Honor and protection included refusing to kill animals and other living things for food or sport, refusing to erect buildings and monuments on every available patch of green grass, and recognizing our contributions to crises like global warming and species extinction. The rest of creation is just as important to God as humanity, and we can't allow the power we have over it to destroy what God made.

I could rock with that. The more I read scholarship within the discipline, the more it intrigued me, and I tried to do better. I even reached out to my friends Dustin and Leah for vegan recipes. (It still surprises me I'll take fried cauliflower over chicken wings. And while that is a major accomplishment, I still have to pray for grace because after Leah gave me the rawest veggie pita I've ever had in my life, I can't see living my days without pepperoni.) But spending time unpacking the powerful act of creating the world reoriented my understanding of the relationship God has with creation and challenged me to think less about humanity having dominion over things. Creation care also pushed me toward honoring the interdependence creation is supposed to have with itself. Earth and humanity need each other. God created them both with intention. The moment we begin to think of one part as more important than the other, we've missed it. So creation care provided me with new language and ways to explore our food consumption as a holy practice and protecting the land and vulnerable species as acts of worship. I got it.

But the more I studied about creation and became intentional about how we should care for it, the more it began to sink in that Black people are part of creation, too. Most of the scholars talking in this lane were White and I hadn't yet been introduced to Black scholars and practitioners like Derek Hicks at Wake Forest University and Pastor Heber Brown in Baltimore who were doing this work. While caring for the land and sentient beings is important, these White scholars weren't making room in their scholarship to discuss the treatment of Black people. And if they weren't talking about Black folk, I knew they weren't checking for Black women. The racism and dehumanization Black bodies experience run contrary to God's intention for creation. Additionally, exploring creation care theology began to give me the language I was looking for those years ago when I declared to my mama that the Black Church was sexist. It helped me to articulate how Black women aren't seen as part of creation. They aren't automatically marked by God as "good" (according to the preachers Mama and I grew up hearing) and, thus, would have to earn that holy distinction. My analysis still needed some work before I could fully convey it to people, and I would talk it over with my friends so it could become even more clear to me. But I knew it was in the doctrine of creation where I would situate the most important argument I'd ever make: if all of creation is holy, then Black girls and women are holy, too.

As a nurse, Mama already had an ethic of creation care by which she believed in our interdependency with other parts of the created world. The more my analysis grew, the more she joked I would follow in her footsteps and she just might get a nurse for a daughter after all. She knew my lane wasn't nursing or anything medical but she was excited this exploration would lead me to a healthier understanding of God and a healthier life.

In the years since, I've explored these questions in further detail—in my blog writings, in my social media rants, and in discourse and debate with my colleagues and other theologians. Where did Christians get the idea we are these wretched creatures who need so desperately to be thrown the bone of salvation for our lives to have any value or meaning? Sure, these sentiments are reiterated in sermons and songs, but where did they come from and why do we believe them? At what point did we decide to begin our relationship with God with sin when that's not where God starts it?

The way I read it, the work of creation was an act of love. This omniscient, omnipresent, sustaining force took the time to make one of the most significant things it ever would. The Holy Maker called every single aspect of the design "good." It was good. It was right, majestic, glorious, beautiful, and in need of no tweaks and reconstructions. When God looked at creation, God saw necessary perfection. God saw a good thing.

Necessary perfection, being a good thing, doesn't mean we are perfect. Just as God saw the totality of creation as good, God also knew creation would be trifling. Humanity. People. People would be trifling. People *are* trifling—doing the most with the absolute least. And yes, the biblical narrative is replete with examples of humanity fumbling the ball and God extending grace and mercy. We can look to our own lives and see where God has done the same thing. Yet, that doesn't change the fact that God has seen us as only one thing since the beginning: good.

It's hard to reflect on the time I didn't believe I was deserving of my mother's love and had, somehow, tainted her. I don't know what parts of me were fed by believing such foolishness but it starved my self-worth. And it robbed me of moments I could have been making more beautiful memories with her. When we force ourselves to deny our original goodness, we lose. Believing the lie that we were insufficient before we encountered Christ only takes away from us. It never adds. It festers and seeps through us, contaminating so much. For whatever reason, there were folks in my family and in my church who wanted me to be less than what I have always been. They wanted me to walk in an inferiority I gladly welcomed. And maybe "gladly" is too harsh for even myself. Perhaps I just didn't know any better at the time. Now I do.

We are good creation because God says we are. Full stop.

We are not perfect. At best, we are stumbling along trying to make sense of the world and our place in it. We will make mistakes along the way. We will forget we are inherently good and will lean into the desperation that accompanies believing otherwise. In doing so, we will hurt ourselves and others. This will grieve God's heart and, even then, we will still be good. At the very worst moments of our lives, we will still put a twinkle in God's eye because God knows who we truly are.

Mama's refusal to stand in front of a congregation and repent for being pregnant was the first step she took in raising me to believe I am enough. My refusal to accept that I—and anyone else for that matter—was born in sin and shaped in iniquity was the first step I took in knowing it to be true.

SUING GOD FOR BACK
CHILD SUPPORT

For years, I believed Luther Vandross was my daddy and my mama had no intention of telling me otherwise. She didn't listen to secular music much but, whenever Luther came on, life stopped for her. On one of our annual summer vacations to Las Vegas, "So Amazing" blared through the lobby of our hotel. Mama stopped everything and sang the entire song in full voice. I didn't necessarily believe her "Luther is your daddy" declarations, but I figured anyone who could get my mama to sing publicly about anybody but Jesus was somebody important.

Ironically, some church drama would force Mama to "confess" I would not inherit Luther's fortune. The search for a new pastor can be a contentious time in the life of a church. The power a seat on the search committee holds often makes friendly members bitter rivals. It can show you very clearly who is believed to be saved and who is not. As a member of our church's pastoral search committee, Mama became one of the people folks quickly decided they didn't like. It didn't matter that they'd worked alongside each other for years in Zion Hill Missionary Baptist Church and were raising children together there. Once Mama was a member of the pastoral search committee, all bets were off. She wasn't their friend and fellow church member anymore. She was someone who had the ability to determine who would, ultimately, become the pastor. And when she voted in a way they didn't like, she became a target.

At the time, one of my cousins worked with a few of our church members. Like her mother, she didn't really care much for my mother then. My cousin overheard Mama talking with Grandma about the latest church happenings, went back to work, added a few things to spice up the story, and all hell broke loose. One evening, Mama called me into her room and showed me a letter she'd received in the mail that day. It said she had no business trying to represent a congregation when she'd had a baby out of wedlock. Obviously in a hurry to get the letter in the mail before the following Sunday, the writer didn't even bother to get a new envelope. Instead, they used an envelope intended for something else. Having already put a return address on it, they just placed a yellow label over it and addressed the envelope to Mama like normal. She pulled back the label so I could see who wrote the letter. It would be years before I found a way to let it go and forgive them.

Sitting me on the edge of her bed, Mama told me several things. First, she told me I couldn't return to Zion Hill until things cooled down. I'd have to go to church with my grandma. While I loved St. Stephen Missionary Baptist Church, I was devastated. But the politics of church business, and the ugliness it brought out of people, meant Zion Hill was no longer safe for me. I wanted Mama to leave. She could come back to St. Stephen or we could find another church. We'd never have to see those people again. I begged her. But Mama said, "God doesn't get the glory that way." She said, "You get the victory when you stand toe-to-toe with the devil and refuse to back down."

For months, Mama went to church with very few friends and without me. I hated anyone who didn't like her, including my cousin. All these people were mean and, because things weren't going their way, they didn't care that a child was caught in the crossfire. They didn't care that they used a child to harm and shame a grown woman. I may have been upset about having to go to St. Stephen, but it was a blessing. While before I may have only heard whispers or seen disapproving glances during accusatory sermons, this situation pulled the veil off people's disrespect. Now it was impossible to ignore what they *really* thought about Mama and me.

The evening Mama showed me the letter from our church member, she said she wanted to tell me about my father before someone else did and added whatever they wanted to for humiliation's sake. Although I'd only seen him in the grocery store parking lot but instantly knew it was him, Mama and I hadn't yet had a full heart-to-heart about the circumstances of their relationship. I'd been too young then and, as a twelve-year-old, I was still too young for certain parts of it. But I didn't have the heart to tell her she was too late. Adults, at church and in my family, had intentionally whispered in my earshot in hopes I'd go back and repeat to her what I heard.

By the time my mother told me about my father, I'd met him once. Mama and I were coming out of the grocery store and a man whose cocoa complexion put me in mind of my grandfather was entering. When he saw me, he smiled at me in a way no man had ever smiled at me before. It was then I knew. He spoke to my mother. She was polite, spoke back, and we kept walking. Though the man had been on his way into the grocery store, he followed us to our car. Their conversation grew tense. He kept asking questions. Mama kept responding with one-word answers. Responding to questions with one-word answers was akin to cursing in my house, so I knew whoever this man was, he had the power to rattle my mother. Seeing Mama become a bit unsettled confirmed who this man was for me. When I climbed in the back of our Festiva, he put his hand on the window and smiled at me again. My smile matched his, in size and shape.

When we were pulling out of the parking lot, Mama asked me one question: "Do you know who that is?"

"My daddy."

Mama pressed the brakes and asked me if I wanted to talk to him. I don't know what made him turn around but, when he saw the brake lights, he began walking back to the car. As I looked out the rearview mirror watching this man who'd walked out so many years ago now walk back to me, something in me knew he wouldn't stay. "No. I want to go home." I watched him watch us drive away and wondered what he could be thinking. Did he expect me to talk to him? Was he sad? Was he mad at me?

We didn't go home. Ma drove fifteen minutes out of the way to the Baskin-Robbins on Peters Creek Parkway. She got her beloved butter pecan and let me get the rainbow sherbet on a sugar cone I didn't even ask for. That alone made the moment special. Asking Mama if I could get a sugar cone was like asking for a million dollars. In later years, she'd joke and say it was her way of keeping me humble because going to Baskin-Robbins was a treat in itself and she didn't want me to become spoiled. We both laughed at how serious she was and ridiculous she sounded.

Driving back home, Mama asked me if I was okay. I told her the truth. I didn't know. I dreamt of my father. Even though part of me knew Mama was just playing about Luther, I fantasized my dad was equally important. He was on some secret mission for the government and the reason he wasn't coming around was for our safety. Or he'd been kidnapped by foreign spies and was fighting every day to get back to me. I constantly created these wild and impossible conspiracy theories because they were better than the truth: he didn't want me. Of course, I wanted to know him. But seeing him in that grocery store parking lot, I couldn't bring myself to *make* the decision that I would get to know him. Coming to that conclusion was too much responsibility and, even at nine, I knew it wasn't my responsibility. Even if I said yes to my mama, it would have been me making the decision to talk to him. He wouldn't have done anything to see me. He'd bumped into me running in to buy some milk or chicken legs and I believed I deserved more. I wanted him to make the effort to come and see me.

Years before she passed, Mama and I would talk about the night I met my father and she took me for ice cream. I was surprised she remembered it. She said it was the night she realized she couldn't control whether I'd want a relationship with him. Up to then, she was protecting me. He wanted to be in and out of my life, by way of her bed, and she couldn't afford the pain his inconsistency would cause me or her. Instead, she drew a line in the sand. Because he didn't actually want to be a father, he couldn't have access to me. But in the parking lot, Mama said she saw in my eyes how much I wanted him and, if I would've told her I wanted to spend time with him, she knew she couldn't say no. She was right. Had I asked to see my father and Mama told me no, I would have believed *she* was keeping me from him. We wouldn't have gotten past it and that tension would have always been present between us, rehashed during every major fight or disagreement.

Despite fantasies of my father being Luther Vandross or some kind of covert agent, I had a man who wanted to be my dad. Right around the time I turned one, Mama began dating a man, Hubert Hill, who accepted me as his daughter. He died less than two years later, and I don't think my mother's heart ever recovered. Still, Hubert was Daddy to me. I grew up with his father being my grandpa Bud, his mother my grandma Sarah, and his brother and sisters were my uncle and aunts. Though we don't have a close relationship, his biological son and I consider each other family and it's love each time we see each other. To this day, Hubert's nieces and nephews are just as much my cousins as the Benbows, Carters, and Pledgers. I have a massive picture of Hubert that his sister, my aunt Theresa, gave me, and I often joked with my mother that I was going to get a painter to create a custom drawing of the two of them together to hang over my fireplace. A million times over, I have imagined what my life would have been had he not died. I dreamt he would have married my mom, and I would've had the family she wanted for me. And, even if they divorced and went on to separate lives and new loves, he would not have divorced me. I would have always been his baby girl.

I longed to be a daddy's girl. The fact it was not in the cards for me was heartbreaking. Be clear—I knew and know fatherly love. The adoration I received from Grandaddy and Grandpa Bud, at times, felt extra because they knew I needed more than their other grandchildren. Two of my mother's brothers, Derrick and Dean, remain constant presences in my life. They're the first I call when there's a problem and, on some level, I expect them to fix it. And from my pastor to male mentors and men from my church and youth programs, there are men who have stepped up to father me. Honorable men have been consistent presences in my life; Mama made sure of it. Still, there were moments when I just wanted my dad. Where was he? Why would so many other men want to be part of my life but my father refuse to be? Why didn't he go to court and get visitation? Why didn't he demand my mother allow him to see me? Why didn't he help her with me? Why didn't he want me?

Sitting on the bed, holding what had been the meanest letter I'd ever read in my life, Mama told me everything I wanted to know about my father. Before that night a few years prior, I didn't know much about him. Luther's face was his. Now I knew what he looked like and had begun to obsess over how much I looked like him. My mother made the promise, no matter what I asked her about their relationship, she'd tell me the truth—even if it shed an unfavorable light on her in my eyes. And she did. Through tears, she told me everything. If she said something I didn't understand, she broke it down until I got it. But there was nothing my mother could have done wrong in my eyes, then or now. She wasn't perfect. None of us are. But Mama stayed; he didn't. Her commitment to me would always elevate her word over his. Even as a child I knew any person who doesn't take care of their responsibilities isn't someone to be trusted. My father had a whole child living in the world whom he didn't acknowledge or support. Such behavior didn't make him a paragon of honesty and integrity to me.

Mama refused to speak negatively about my father and I couldn't understand it. I actually hated it. Throughout the years, when I would randomly ask her a question, she'd respond as if this man had given her a million dollars. Once, I asked her why she didn't make him pay child support. "I refused to go downtown and let a judge know I was a fool for some man." I knew Mama hated him; she had to. Why couldn't she just show it to me? "There's a lot about him that you don't understand. He doesn't even understand it. But it doesn't matter because God had to get you here . . ." Rarely did she go off script. The same woman who wanted me to know I wasn't a mistake and was meant to be here found a way to explain away my father's absence as his inability to comprehend his responsibility as a man and a father, and God's will for his life. She was able to reconcile the two in ways I refused. And she saw my refusal as an inability to let go and truly heal. Maybe she was right. It just seemed to me that God was letting my dad off the hook pretty easily.

I had every reason to hate my father. I was one of three children and he was present in the lives of the other two. Both of my half brothers knew him and lived with him. While my younger brother grew up in St. Stephen and I knew him, I went to high school with my older brother and hated it. During my freshman year at Parkland Senior High School, Mama took me to a Friday night football game and, refusing to be seen with her (you know how it is with teenagers), I immediately ditched her to find my friends. When we got home, she sat me down and told me she'd run into my father's brother at the game with his nephew, my brother. My head was reeling. It was the first time I was learning about having an older brother. When I told him this, he made a scene, called my mother a "ho," and I hated him for the rest of the time I was in high school. Granted, we were kids and he was just finding out about me too, but I would have killed him if my friend and classmate Brandon Bowman hadn't held me against the gate and kept me away from him.

Seeing my brother in school was a painful daily reminder that our father chose not to be in my life. Once, I went to the main office of our high school at the same time my dad came to pick up my brother. When he saw me, he said, "Tell your mama to call me." His smug arrogance provoked me to reply,

"I'll tell her to kick your ass!" Before school ended for the day, our main secretary, Ms. McDonald, called me back to the office. A Black woman, she pulled me aside and told me to never give anybody, especially a man, the power to pull me out of character. I apologized and told her it wouldn't happen again. She promised not to tell my mother. I told Mama anyway and was grounded for a month for being disrespectful.

Between Mama being nice when it came to my father and me being placed on punishment for cursing him out, I didn't understand the relentless negative impact of my dad's actions on *my* life. And I struggled to pray about it. In my mind, God was a man, and men stuck together. God would look out for my dad and cosign his foolishness because that's what men do. After all, God was only referred to as "He" and "Him" in church and in the scriptures. Add to that the trifling things I'd heard men—pastors included—had done and gotten away with. God was on the side of his homeboys.

To this day, I've seen men lie for each other, gaslight the hell out of women to make us second-guess ourselves and our own common sense—all to protect their boy. I saw it when the men would assist each other in the creation and perpetuation of false alibis. And it was up close and personal for me when I got my heart broken and men I deeply respected said, "Well . . . maybe you misconstrued some things." What I *haven't* seen are men en masse challenging or critiquing one another about their harmful ways. Granted, I have homeboys and close male friends who are in therapy and doing the work to be well. But they aren't the norm. That's the problem. And, for as much as I want to shout from the rooftops that I am in community with healthy Black men, I think my efforts are far better spent trying to get more men to recognize the need to be well.

I can count on both hands how many times I've talked with my father and multiple fingers remain. There was the time my senior year in high school when I just showed up at my brother's house simply because I wanted to see my father. He told me things would be different, that he would be a better father. It never happened. There was the time I came home for spring break and he stood me up at Olive Garden. I was crying so uncontrollably the waiter had to take my phone and talk to Mama. My dad called a few days later and, for a reason I can't seem to remember, got snippy with me. Mama took the phone and said her piece. Then there was the time he told me he didn't really want me. He doesn't remember saying it and adamantly denies it. And, to be fair, he said it in the context of not considering himself ready to be a father (although he was already one), but I will never forget it. It's quite impossible to erase from your memory the day your father confirmed your worst fears.

And then there was Christmas 2019, when I thought we'd turned over a new leaf and he would do better. He said he would. Instead, it was more of the same; except, this time, it felt much more painful and intentional. This was the first year I knew his actual birthday and called him with well wishes. He didn't answer nor did he return the call. And, as the COVID-19 pandemic rocked the world in 2020, he didn't pick up the phone once to check on me. Even after his refusals to care for me, I still called him in October 2020, as I was preparing to buy my first car on my own. In my mind, fathers assist their daughters with major purchases and, considering Mama was gone, I knew he would take this opportunity to finally step up. Instead, I got a string of excuses and a promise to call me in a few days to let me know what he could do. The next call I received was on Thanksgiving, inviting me to eat dinner with him and offering to pick me up from my grandmother's house if I needed a ride. By that time, I'd had my new car for over a month.

As soon as I came of age, I had to come to terms with the fact that my father is trifling as hell. And praying he'd change felt counterintuitive. I believed God heard my prayers about everything else but, when we got to my dad, God must have fallen asleep and didn't hear those. Looking back, I think I wanted some kind of tangible sign that my father was suffering because he wasn't present in my life. There should have been nothing good happening for him; he didn't deserve goodness. That he was thriving in my eyes—simply because he was breathing—confirmed my suspicions: God and my father were conspiring against me.

Even though preachers and singers would say God is "a mother to the motherless," it was understood the Creator of Heaven and Earth is male. Scripture backed it up. Male pronouns are used throughout the bible and, if that didn't make it clear, Jesus refers to God as *his Father*. I laugh about it now—and it is absolutely hilarious—but one of my homeboys argued me down that God is a man because Jesus said so. "If you tell me your mother's name is Jessica, why would I call her Stephanie? Why would I do that, Candice?" It was a terrible analogy, but in essence, he was saying because Jesus called God "father" in the bible, that makes God male. But when I asked why God is only described in a way aligning God with one particular aspect of creation, he told me I was being intentionally divisive. That's church code for "you have a point but I don't appreciate it so I'm going to resort to good old-fashioned gaslighting as a redirect."

When discussing the Trinity, some male theologians and pastors attempt to pacify women by saying the Holy Spirit is feminine. Some would argue it represents how the Trinity balances masculine and feminine energies to "produce" Jesus but it still feels off. It's like saying, "Okay, yall, the Holy Spirit is a woman. Yall comfort and are present and do the nurturing stuff it does. Happy now?" Even with this, what is to be wholly accepted is God came to Earth with a penis and that male form has been the object of worship for more than two thousand years. And people think that's crass. But when you honestly sit with it, the bible's continual reference to God using "Father" and "Son" and "He" reinforces the idea God is male.

Even though I had come to terms with the patriarchal and sexist foundations of Western Christianity and how it functions in the Black Church while still in undergrad, I didn't fully understand how wedded I remained to those notions until I got to Duke and professors required we use inclusive language for God—which meant abandoning gendered pronouns and using "God" and "Godself." What I was doing on paper, I pushed myself to do in real life. Thinking of God outside of a gendered perspective made God less limited to me. And it made God less common. While God desires to be close to us and is, there was something about using the same pronouns for God I use for every other man in my life that felt less holy to me. And therefore, ungendering God restored so much of God's majesty and wonder to me. Considering my spiritual path, inclusive language pushed me to create an ethic to honor the ways I was growing and shifting.

Folks weren't having it, though. I didn't even think many would notice but once, while teaching bible study, I only used God and Godself during the lesson. Afterward, my pastor told me such a move wasn't the "culture" of the church and I needed to understand that everything I was learning in seminary wasn't appropriate for the congregation. For many, to question God's maleness is to question the power of men. And when Black men have found an unlimited supply of power within the Black Church, what could possibly get them to give that up? It's not difficult to find women who support them and justify their positions, either. To tell the truth, this was one of the areas where my mother and I fought constantly. I believed her insistence on God's masculinity was what enabled her to make excuses for a man who abandoned her with a child—that she saw God in an absentee father more than she saw God in herself. She believed I went to Duke, read two books, and lost my mind; and she told me I had one more time to say another disrespectful thing to her before she sent me to meet God and I would be able to see the gender for myself.

I eased up on the rhetoric because Mama didn't play but I stood firm in my heart and my thinking. I could no longer unsee the danger in assigning gender to God. Beyond just saying God is a man, assigning the male gender to God potentially shapes how we, especially Black Christians, see *all* men. It creates structures which assert only men are capable of leading. It sustains hierarchy, making all but cisgender, heterosexual men bottom-feeders. And because our communities feel the need to affirm straight Black men and help them navigate racism at the expense of the rest of us, suggesting a shift toward an ungendered God barely stands a chance.

Families, churches, schools—in each sphere, you can find routine uplifting of "good Black men"—really just men who leaned a little more into respectability politics than their brethren—because they *could* be off somewhere doing other things. The bar for Black masculinity is so low we celebrate Black men simply because they're not robbing, raping, and wreaking economic and physical havoc. It doesn't matter if their good-guy routine is a ruse enabling them to be bad men in secret. They're good men in public and that's what matters. And truth be told, we've seen men work their way around being trifling publicly—especially when they're in the church.

My father wasn't held accountable for being an unwed parent like my mother was. And, throughout the years he was active in congregations, he was deeply beloved. As a member of the choir, he led songs, and people looked to him with great respect. It didn't matter that his role in my life was nonexistent. There was no accountability for him. Is there ever? How are we supposed to account for men who are absent fathers and all-around terrible guys and yet still seem to find folks to tell them it's okay, the people they hurt will understand how social and structural pressures caused them to make the decisions they did? How are women supposed to react when they see men who've hurt them finally "get it together," and be told it's the responsibility of the people they hurt to let it go and see them for who they are now and not who they used to be? My response: membership has its privileges.

For years, I refused the term "daddyless daughter." I'm actually not one. I have a dad; he's just trifling. And his refusal to actively parent me manifested itself in me in ways that will probably take a lifetime to overcome. It would be years before I understood that the shame I associated with being my mother's daughter was actually rooted in the sorrow of not being my father's daughter. I believe it is the parent's responsibility to ensure their child is healthy, whole, and able to thrive. For some, giving their children up for adoption so they could be raised by others who could give them a safe and better life or sending their children back to the spirit realm, through abortion, because they weren't ready to parent are the best ways to live into that parental responsibility. But that's not the decision my father made and no number of explanations or excuses will justify his or any parent's willful neglect. And the trauma has a ripple effect across other relationships. Because my father is a piss-poor dad, my brothers and I are essentially strangers. Despite our now being adults who can choose to have relationships with each other apart from our father, it's still quite difficult. They believe I owe him more respect. I feel he's lucky he gets what he does. This isn't their fault or mine. We have different relationships with him, which produce different perspectives. In the end, our estrangement is a casualty of his absence.

When it comes to my relationship with my father, I can't tell you how many times I've heard "Let it go." Letting go, without accountability, is somehow proof of healing. I've been told to accept my father for who he is, even if it means I must shoulder the responsibility of initiating and sustaining our relationship on my own. But that advice doesn't honor the truth of my experience, of what I've wanted and needed in a dad. At nine, I knew I deserved a father who put forth the effort to be my father. Thirty years later, I still know that. In part, ungendering God also freed me from the idea God has favorites and my dad was one of them. God loves my father, without a doubt. And God is disappointed in my father and other absent parents for abandoning their children and responsibilities. I needed to understand that—it mattered significantly to me.

There are progressive theologies which describe God as a woman. In the beginning, I needed them. I needed to read *The Shack* and see God portrayed as a Black woman. I needed to read womanist theologians like Delores S. Williams, Jacquelyn Grant, M. Shawn Copeland, and others who troubled God's gender for me. Their work gave me a framework to expand my understanding of God. Truth be told, if anybody asked me to describe God in human form, I would describe my mama. She gave me life and saved it a thousand times over, nurtured me through correction and compassion. In my life, she is God enfleshed. On some level, I would have always understood God as a woman, as a *Black* woman. I think if we described God with the human attributes of the person who has cared for us the most in this life, our renderings would look different from the God given to us. Perhaps that's the point. When God wrapped Godself in Brown flesh and became Jesus, divinity came in a form no one expected or initially appreciated. Maybe God is to be that personal to us. Christ, who is both God's son and Godself, challenged the way the people of his time understood what God could look like. We must have the courage to do the same.

Even though I needed to see God as a woman to begin healing from the harm of masculine-centered theologies, I've since shifted away from expressing God through gender altogether. Now, you'll still see me rocking my "I Met God . . . She's Black" T-shirt proudly. I love it because it's true. Black women have been God for me more times than I can count. (Plus, I absolutely love how the declaration pisses White people and Black men off.) Admittedly, I still slip up and have to catch myself when I refer to God with male pronouns. More times than not, it's done with friends to spoof the masculinity-drenched Black Church. And I've slid it in a few times when I've preached to certain congregations because I understand my audience. But, honestly, old habits die hard. For more than thirty years, God was male to me. Certain belief systems don't disappear overnight no matter how hard I try or how many books I read. With sincere intention, in public writing and speech, I refer to God as God because I resist the allure of entangling God in the same bondage I needed God freed from.

For me, God's love makes the difference. What do I lose when I ungender God? I abandon the notion that there are some who are outside of God's identity and, therefore, God's love. I lose the claim I stake in believing this is the right and only way to know God. And I grab hold of the reality that the vast conceptions of the human existence can be found within God. This has opened a path for even greater explorations of God's nature that are mindful of queer, trans, nonbinary, and gender-nonconforming folks. Pushing beyond the limits of gender and language construction helps us to discover how expansive God truly is. Moving the concept of God outside of the box it has been in also scares people to the point of believing it's heretical and demonic. I've watched Christians who consider themselves to be LGBTQIA+ affirming and progressive absolutely lose it when someone says God is queer. But doesn't such a declaration really just affirm God's desire for a more inclusive and compassionate creation? All humanity can be exists within God. Who are we, with our finite understanding, to say how endless those possibilities are?

God is God. God created all things, exists beyond time, and is eternal. God stood before language or identity and is not defined by them. God is compassionate and empathetic enough to make room for us to come to know God as we need to come to know God. While I think it gave us an initial point of reference, the push to understand God through gendered language does not come from the Divine. It comes from our need to control, to lay claim, to create proximity to those whose authority we believe shouldn't be questioned. But domination is not God's will for us. God pushes and nudges us toward more freeing, liberating ways to see the Holy because, when we shift our gaze, we welcome true intimacy and connection. Because, more than anything, God desires relationship with us.

While facilitating Oprah Winfrey's Lifeclass in 2011, Iyanla Vanzant worked with a young man who could not let go of the animosity he had toward his absent father. Iyanla suggested that, instead of focusing on the anger, the young man should express gratitude because his father "lent his body back to God" so he could have life. Immediately, I thought of the times my mother told me God had to get me here however God could. Yet I hadn't considered honoring my father's role in the act of creating me. So much of my time had been focused on reeling from the fact that he was not active in the physical realm that I'd not expressed gratitude for what my father did in the spirit realm. And perhaps my mother was right. Maybe there are reasons I will never know or understand which kept and keep my father from being who he's supposed to be to me. My prayer is, while I honor my father's holy offering, he has found a way to offer up his own life for the sake of himself. There is grace for my father, even if he doesn't take it. And there is grace for me as I navigate my own angst and frustrations. While I doubt we will ever understand each other, God understands us both.

The God who is real holds my father accountable for his absence in my life just as God holds me accountable for the ways I have lived contrary to my ethics and integrity. This God isn't creating structures to hold me more responsible for the things I've done because I "should've known better" while creating an exhaustive list of reasons why my dad simply couldn't be the man he was supposed to be. The God who worked, with intention and care, to bring creation to life has called humanity to be its highest self. This God moves with and is moved by us. The moment we shift from this truth is the moment we are no longer connected to God.

GOD AND OTHER REFORMED
HELICOPTER PARENTS

We'd been arguing for thirty minutes over my Facebook post. I had a penchant for living my Black feminist ideals and beliefs out loud on social media. I took a screenshot of a rape threat DMd to me after a tense public exchange with a notable pastor and posted it on Facebook. Once she saw it, Mama called me immediately. She told me to come home. I was living an hour away in Durham, North Carolina, at the time and had plans. I wasn't coming. She then told me to delete my social media profiles. I laughed.

"If you don't stop antagonizing these people on social media, I'm going to have to take matters into my own hands."

"And do what?"

Now, I was talking big junk because I was on the phone and wasn't heading home. To be fair, Mama had a lot of ways she could've taken matters into her own hands. She bought my cars. She was paying my rent and utilities, leaving my salary to be my "play money." She could have easily told me I had to pay for my own life, and I would've been distraught. But, as frustrated as my mama was with me then (and so many times before and after), she knew I was becoming my own person, and was going to do what I wanted to do despite her objections.

I am fundamentally different from my mother. Where I'm more wild and outgoing, Mama was definitely more reserved. To explain our differences when I was growing up, she would joke and tell me she found me in a cabbage patch. She would also share with other parents how, once she got to know me, she learned very quickly whuppings wouldn't work as punishment. As a kid, I didn't understand what she meant by "once she got to know me." Didn't she *always* know me? I was *her* daughter. When I got older, I understood that Mama recognized our differences and realized who she thought I was going to be was not who I was becoming, and I needed space and room to grow into myself. Besides adjusting her discipline style, she would allow me to say what kinds of activities I was interested in versus simply putting me in some just because she wanted to. When I told her I didn't want to take dance anymore but I wanted to join the city's youth debate team, she initially said no. But when we pulled up to the library for debate practice instead of the dance studio, I was glad she heard me. And while I would much rather have taken a whupping than been restricted to "Emergency Communication Only" for a month, I appreciated her genuine effort to better know her child.

The more I grew into my voice, the more comfortable I became talking about my exploits in front of her. On Facebook,

I didn't hide posts or change the tenor of conversations because she was one of my "friends." And she hated it! I told her social media was for millennials and, if Boomers were going to encroach on our space, they'd have to deal with whatever conversations took place. I used to joke and tell Mama she raised me to be double-minded and unstable. On one hand, she took me to the library every Friday to check out a book by a Black woman and took me to public lectures on feminism at her alma mater, Winston-Salem State, as well as Wake Forest University and Salem College. On the other hand, she told me there are three things a lady must never discuss in public: sex, religion, and politics. She'd raised a daughter whose desired career required public conversations about all three. But just because I was becoming my own woman didn't mean I gave up on being who my mama wanted me to be. Walking the line between those two ideals, at times, felt impossible.

I talk a lot about my mother's choice to raise me in church because, aside from school, church is where I spent the bulk of my time outside the home. Many of my enrichment programs were housed in a church. When Mama wanted me in a Black Girl Scout troop, she and a few other moms in our congregation started one. I knew my address, my grandma's, and the address of Zion Hill Missionary Baptist Church by heart. Church was where I developed many of my leadership skills. But being raised in church doesn't necessarily just mean being raised in faith.

Instead of just learning about Jesus and how we can be better people in the world, we were going to church to be groomed so we would be better than the kids not in church. If educated Black folks were the talented tenth, saved Black folks were the "Elect," and saved children were their inheritance. Church and holy-rolling family members privileged us and held us in higher regard than kids who spent less time in church and more time on, to let Saints tell it, "the streets." We thought we were better because church folk told us we were. It was such an odd tension—to try to find ways to wield power as a "good, godly child" given to me by the very system which denigrated the circumstances of my birth. But each of us was doing that dangerous dance, including women who had no real institutional power but held the line for holiness and made sure to let you know when you didn't meet it.

But we were kids being pitted against other kids. As long as we stayed in God's hand and did what God told us to do, we would be blessed. Church leaders made us religious zealots before we even had time to form our own thoughts about God and faith. I believed if I wasn't like the "fast" girls I would go far. My dreams were contingent upon me keeping my legs closed and staying focused. I was sizing up girls in middle and high school, determining their prospects for success based on whatever gossip lingered about them. But I wasn't the only one who thought like this. And part of our confusion, right now, is trying to understand how we ended up in the same place they did or with them ahead of us.

When our religious communities were telling us to do what God said, they were actually telling us to do what *they* said. And, on some level, I get it. Our lens for reading and interpreting scripture doesn't just drop out of the sky or appear by osmosis. Our faith is crafted and expressed within com-

munity. Black folk have long looked for ways to escape oppression. Christians believed they found the only way. If we
acted according to God's Holy Word, everything was within
our grasp. The husband and the children—because, let's face
it, that's all most of us wanted anyway—could be ours. We
would inherit the keys to the kingdom. Consequently, *everything* was considered a "sin." Born and raised Baptist, I don't
recall hearing an actual definition of "sin" growing up—just
examples of it. Smoking was a sin. Drinking was a sin. Cursing
was a sin. Having sex outside of marriage was *the* sin. But although Christians said these behaviors were sinful, no one
ever explained *why* they were—nor could they explain why
many Christians still engaged in them.

All I knew was Adam and Eve introduced sin into the
world. Well, actually, it was just Eve. The biblical writer says
God told the pair they could have anything in the Garden of
Eden but couldn't eat fruit from the Tree of the Knowledge of
Good and Evil. The serpent tricked Eve by, essentially, telling
her God lied to them about what would happen if they ate it.
Eve bit the fruit. When Adam saw Eve eating the fruit up, he
said "YOLO," and took a bite. You would think this is the first
moment of romantic solidarity—showing Adam to be ride or
die. If Eve is going down, then he's going down with his baby,
too. But that went out the window in Genesis 3:12, when God
rolled up, and Adam blamed his actions on "the woman you
gave me." Have you ever heard any of the "We must protect
our Black queens" preachers talk about the fact that Adam did
the exact opposite? Let me take a wild guess.

But it was thanks to the original parents that sin entered

the world. And, what was their "punishment" or consequence? They got kicked out of the garden, Eve was cursed
with labor pains, and Adam was forced to work hard. Let me
get this straight. After doing the one thing God told them not
to do, Eve and all the women who come after her have to endure PMS, heavy flows, menstrual cramps and, if they're lucky
to birth children (or even want to), they have to go through
horrendous and possibly life-ending pain, and the only thing
men have to do is get a job and actually do it well—and even
then, they still crafted the world in their favor so they wouldn't
have to. If you ask me, Eve and women got the short end of
this stick. It didn't sit right with me how the original parents
were given everything and then told they couldn't have one
thing placed in the midst of it. Why was the tree even there?
Ain't it common knowledge you want the very thing you
can't have? I didn't have to eat from a tree to know that. Why
was God setting them up like this? In the immortal, now GIFd,
words of Cardi B: What was the reason?

I've heard tons of explanations. God put the tree there
to test their faith—to see if they understood they needed to
totally rely on God. That seems ridiculous. Faith is tested
through trials and hard times, not entrapment. Others taught
us the Tree of the Knowledge of Good and Evil possessed information only God needed to know. But if God was the only
being who needed the knowledge, why was the tree in the garden? I don't leave my social security number and debit card
lying around in reach of anyone. It's just for me. And others
simply said the tree was there "because God said so" and we
can't question God. This sounds good in theory but it is yet

another example of church folk telling me to do what *they* said and pretending it's what God said. I just refused to believe I couldn't ask questions. Even if my questions went unanswered more times than not, nothing would keep me from asking them. And I know I'm not the only one.

To be honest, when it comes to the events in the garden, I thought God did the most. Controversial and, in some spaces, downright blasphemous to say, I don't see "punishing" Adam and Eve as one of God's shining moments. As a result of one "mistake," humankind was automatically rendered broken and fallen. But have we ever stopped to think if God was really right? Was what actually happened, as a result of eating the fruit, *that* bad? Was this an instance of God believing God knew best and refusing Adam and Eve the space to grow?

A few years in Sunday School, bible study, and prayer meeting and you learn very quickly God's wrath toward the original Bonnie and Clyde was justified. I struggled to believe it. And after years of ingesting the church's argument, I came to understand how the story of God's disappointment in Adam and Eve's actions shapes the way we see ourselves. Whenever we do something wrong, so many of us expect the worst consequences possible and believe we deserve them. Some of us can talk about being deserving of God's wrath more than we can ever speak to deserving God's love.

Many refer to God as "father." Since I use inclusive language for God, I recognize God as the "ultimate parent." Parents and guardians often believe they know what's best for us all the time. And there are times when they do. When we are children, there are unseen dangers to us; their protection is essential. And even after I became an adult, there were times when Mama knew better about particular people and certain situations than I did. Yet, if we are honest, there are times when our parents forbade us from doing something simply because they didn't want us to do it. They may have said it was to protect us but it wasn't about our protection at all. The decision to keep us away from a thing was rooted in their own brokenness and fear. There were times when our parents held us back from doing something because who we'd be after we did it didn't necessarily match who they wanted us to be.

While I knew my mama wanted the best for me, what she said or believed about a thing often dislodged my own intuitive knowing about God and who we're meant to be. She vehemently disagreed, but that didn't stop me from believing that in the Garden of Eden God blew up like an overbearing parent—unwilling to allow Adam and Eve to live their own lives. I mean, can we *finally* agree the "punishment" of kicking Adam and Eve out of the garden didn't necessarily fit the "crime"? Imagine your parents kicking you out of the house and cursing you for the rest of your life after you make your first mistake. How is that even healthy? Maybe God did the most and overexaggerated. Maybe God was in God's PMDD window that day because, when those hormones hit, you're liable to do and say anything. It's the only explanation that makes sense to me.

When I get to Heaven and we're walking around a garden far exceeding the beauty and splendor of the first one, I'm going to ask God if God felt like kicking out the OGs was a bit over the top. (I mean, God *did* have a penchant for going a little overboard back in those days—destroying the Earth and regretting humanity and whatnot.) I can't imagine how many times God looked down on Earth, gave a big, heavy Negro sigh, and said, "This never happens on Pluto." So I get it. And because of what I know about God's grace, I'm willing to bet God will say those early years in the creation project were moments where grace and growing pains were limitless. I imagine God will concede the Adam and Eve debacle was one in which the free will God gave humanity was on full display and God just wasn't ready to deal with it.

The concept of "free will" is a tricky one for Christians. Pinning down a definition will depend on your denominational and theological position. Often, Christians associate free will with every terrible choice we've ever made. They'll say leaning into free will means leaning outside God's will and being outside of God's will is "sin." That's how we got to everything remotely pleasurable being sinful, remember?

"What did God say?" If I had a dollar for every time someone posed that four-word question to me—usually in response to my making a decision they deemed rooted in my own agency—I'd be a millionaire. And, because God's voice and the church community's voice were synonymous, inquirers were really asking, "What do you think we'll say or feel about it?" And those questions were both rhetorical. As the "good ones," those of us who grew up in church were regularly cautioned, with biblical justification, against making decisions that went against the grain. Our church teachers used Paul's arguments to tell us doing so would lead us further away from God's intention for us and taint our status in the community. Paul's letters admonished early Christians to recognize the dangers of being led by the flesh. To make decisions for ourselves, according to the church, is to be guided by the flesh and carnal desires. But to run each decision through God is the hallmark of a true Christian and believer. And I wasn't being sarcastic when I asked how and why we'd do that. If I prayed about something and had a good feeling about it, was my intuition confirmation of God's green light? What about the time I was confident that God was pleased with my decision but my mother and others disagreed? Did their dissent mean I was being led by the flesh? How was I supposed to be certain God sanctioned a decision I made?

Honestly, I wasn't one of those "Because God said so" kind of people and I side-eyed them. Even as a child, I knew they were lying. It wasn't that I didn't believe God was talking to folks (although God seemed to be talking to these people a lot about every little thing). I just didn't believe that God was saying what these folks did. Because, too often, God was getting real specific, and sounding like the opinions and judgments of others. It amazed me how much God would tell other people to tell other folks to get their lives together but couldn't tell those same people to mind their own business. The fact that "God's voice" sounded like opinionated Christians telling me what to do made me trust that declarative word from on high even less, largely because trusting it meant teaching me not to trust myself.

Have we ever stopped to examine why we don't trust ourselves? Have we ever considered why it feels impossible to rely on our own intuition and discernment? How did we become so comfortable overspiritualizing our need to lean and depend on God, just masking our fears of our intrinsic feelings, our intrinsic truths?

The more I learned, the more I saw how much fear was present in these spaces. There was a time when I was so scared to say certain choices felt holy to me because they varied greatly from what others deemed to be "God decisions." And, again, I know I'm not the only one. We were sitting on the pews together and it hurts me to see so many of us afraid to bet on ourselves because we see it as betraying God. But how can we truly live without learning to trust ourselves—to trust God *in* ourselves?

There's a real possibility, when we get to Glory, Adam and Eve will tell us they regret what they did. (Well, Adam should always have all the regrets for the way he threw Eve under the bus.) But there's also the very real chance Eve will confess that taking a bite was the best decision she ever made. She may tell us it opened her up to new worlds and possibilities of who she could be and the self-discovery is what mattered. There's a real chance Eve will tell us, if given the opportunity, she would do it over again. That is the power of free will. It's the choice, the freedom to decide on and create the life we want—the life we believe is meant for us and can be ours.

Free will gives us the chance to discover our authentic selves. When we're born, we don't know who we'll actually become. We're shaped and guided by parents, guardians, and those in leadership to become who they think we should be. If we're lucky, we don't get folks who try to dictate the entire process but who guide us as we grow and evolve. Free will, this God-given ability to make choices, allows us to find out who we truly are. Maybe we are inherent risk-takers but grew up being told to play it safe. Or maybe we're introverts who were pushed to be outgoing in ways we didn't want to be. Choosing the truth for ourselves allows us to be self-determinant. It doesn't mean we don't make mistakes or won't look back on some decisions and cringe. What it does mean is, even *with* the fumbles, we're journeying toward a whole and full life.

And be very clear: there is a direct relationship between embracing free will and doing some very dumb shit. When I would find myself in the aftermath of a *terrible* decision, Mama would say, "Now repeat your thought process out loud and see if it sounds as ridiculous to you as it does to me." And it did. I'd be lying if I said every time I *trusted* myself to make good decisions, I actually *made* good decisions. I didn't. Sometimes, I didn't realize they were terrible decisions. Other times, I knew exactly what I was doing, and I knew it was trifling. Either way, I had to lie in the bed I made until I had room to choose differently. I don't romanticize or ignore these moments; I learned something from them. I was foolish plenty of times in my life and I'm sure I'll be foolish again. Where I've learned to be kinder and gentler with myself is accepting there is no real life without making mistakes. Taking the risk to trust myself more means giving myself room to mess up, learn, and readjust.

But free will doesn't only do something for us; I believe it also does something for God. Free will holds God accountable to God's word. We've heard God doesn't lie. At the beginning of the created world, the Godhead desired to make humanity in its image and likeness. Some believe that image and likeness are one of self-determination and an agency embracing who we have the power to become. I'm one of those people. I believe the image of God I bear is the power to speak my life and the worlds I desire to create into existence. It is the authority to name my destiny and work toward it. I believe the same for all of us. And I believe, even when we make decisions other than the ones expected, we are being exactly who God wants us to be. What if our exercise of free will is the measure by which God holds Godself accountable to God's word? We have the ability to make lives of our choosing because they are *our* lives. God gave them to us. The problem is some of us don't fully believe our lives belong to us.

I know what Paul says. I know he's made the idea of being slaves to Christ sound really appealing. But God gave us our lives so we would live them. And God trusts us with the capacity to live them. Just as creation is an act of love, it is also one of trust. God gave us lives because God *trusts* us with them. Knowing the totality of what we are capable of doing and being, God trusts us still. And perhaps, God trusts us because God trusts Godself. If we bear the image of God, then perhaps God trusts we will embody all it personifies.

When you trust someone, you don't expect them to be anything other than who they are. This trips many of us up, myself included. Too often, we have expectations for people beyond their capacity because that's not what they can give and that's not who they are. Not so with God. God doesn't expect us to be anything more than what we are. God expects us to be human. Within that expectation, though, is the hope we will do the right thing and course-correct when we don't. We are on a constant journey of getting it wrong and getting it right. God doesn't expect perfection from us, and yet we place that expectation on ourselves. We do so because, believe it or not, we deem ourselves unworthy. We don't think it's possible God can love us as we are for who we are. And, consequently, we place these unrealistic expectations on ourselves in hopes of living up to and into God's love. And God is looking at us like, "Girl, *what*?" And when we can't live up to the unrealistic expectations, mountains of guilt and shame descend upon us and we can't see ourselves beyond our failures.

When we view ourselves through the lens of Adam and Eve's fall or our own mistakes and awkward moments, then we never truly see ourselves. Think about it. When we think of Adam and Eve, do we think of them in terms of the "worst" thing they did or do we see them as integral parts of creation? When we think about them, do we recognize them as the way sin entered into the world or as God's love made flesh? When we can see them as more than their mistakes, then it's possible to stretch ourselves to consider that eating of the "apple" wasn't a mistake but rather a true sign of their capacity and power. Now, I'm pretty clear I don't view Adam and Eve's entanglement with the fruit as "sin" or "the Fall" but rather a lesson in growing pains. But when I didn't know any better, when everyone around was saying it was sin, how was I supposed to learn to ease up on them so I could ease up on myself?

Mama's acceptance of me and of our fundamental differences didn't mean we didn't fight. When it came to faith and feminism, some moments felt like we were at war. Despite the tension and our theological disagreements, my mother was committed to understanding her child. When she purchased two tubes of MAC's Ruby Woo lipstick—one for me and one for her—a few months before her death, I knew just how committed she was. And her efforts gave me exactly the space I needed to experience new levels of trust—trust in my parent, trust in myself, and trust in God.

Honestly, I don't think what humanity has become is what God had in mind. There's entirely too much destruction and devastation in the world for that to be true. And in the face of so much pain and crisis, what does it mean to trust God? The presence of free will means God understands the range of possibility for our choices. Whatever we choose, I believe God becomes what we need in relationship to the decision made. I've begun to favor the notion that there are *implications* to our choices rather than to frame decisions with the inherently negative connotation of *consequences*. Good and bad choices have implications. I don't subscribe to the belief that there is essentially one "good" choice. I think, given the choices and circumstances in front of us, we strive to make the best decisions we can at the time and adjust to their implications.

Now, I say this knowing full well I made some decisions out of laziness, fear, stubbornness, or simply because I wanted to. And I can admit that the outcomes of those decisions span the range of "this was the best decision I ever made" to "how much Cîroc do I need to consume in my lifetime to forget this?" to Keke Palmer's iconic "I hope I don't sound ridiculous but I don't know who this man is . . . sorry to this man." The point is we have to take ourselves off the hook. The reality with making a choice is we're not going to be able to have all the options presented before us either at once or ever. Making a "good" decision means we've lost out on something just as much as making a "bad" decision means we gained an experience we desired. What does it mean to make a decision you thought was the best you could do at the time and give yourself enough grace to see it as such? I learned to see God's love as that grace. When hindsight becomes perfect vision and I want to go back and do things differently, God's love shapeshifts to enable me to accept the truth: I did what I thought was right at the time for whatever reason and, if faced with the same reality, I will choose differently the next time. Moving away from belief in judgmental consequences concerning my decisions reminds me I'm human. I can choose to trust myself and prepare myself for whatever comes from choosing me.

I don't need a God who knows what I will do before I do it. I am not a robot. I was created with emotions and feelings that can shift in the moment. Plus, I don't think we realize how much our thoughts of predestination and God's omniscience take us off the hook. They make God responsible for our decisions so we don't have to accept any responsibility. I need a God who understands the possibilities of the choices I can make and understands why I make them even if God doesn't agree. And because God trusts me with free will, it comes with great responsibility. I owe it to God and myself to live a life of authenticity. That requires I make decisions true to the core of who I am and that honor me. Sometimes these are not the decisions church people think I should make, and they are not decisions I make in retaliation for years of pent-up frustration and regret. I must be myself. I am righteous, ratchet, intelligent, sensitive, sensual, spiritual, and ambitious. I am an only child who gets tired of people after forty-eight hours. God meets me where I am, in whatever state I'm in, and gives me what I need. The least I can do is give myself the same.

GOD MADE ME BLACK

There were two times in my childhood when I understood very clearly I'm Black.

The first time was during elementary school when Mama and I accidentally drove into a Ku Klux Klan rally. We were in Lexington, North Carolina—one of the most racist towns in our state. As we approached the red light, a line of hooded White people crossed the street in front of us with bullhorns, picket signs, and hate-filled chants. Raised with a healthy knowledge of my history, I knew what those hoods meant and I was scared. Ma looked at me through the rearview mirror. If she was afraid, she didn't make it known. There was no tremble in her voice. "If something happens, run and keep running until you can go into a store and call the police."

Was she crazy? First, how far did she actually think I could run? I wasn't about to get far. And, more important, there was absolutely no way I was leaving her. I'd read enough books and watched enough PBS specials during Black History Month to know what people in those costumes do to people who look like us. If they were going to hurt her, they would have to get through me. Uncle Dean had been taking jujitsu and using me as his test dummy. At the very least, I'd use all the defensive moves he'd shown me if I needed to protect us from the hooded men. Of course I didn't say any of this. "Yes, ma'am."

We watched as the last Klansman walked past our car before Mama sped off. I don't remember if the light was green and I don't remember her ever driving that fast again. But she hit the gas on that Festiva and got us right on out of there. Then we both laughed. We laughed that "White folks are really crazy and we almost died but let's get the hell out of Davidson County" kind of laugh. Later, at home, Mama asked me how I felt about the day. Looking back, I see that she always found a way to make so many of our moments together into after-school specials. I told her I didn't know KKK members were still alive. In my child's mind, I assumed the Klan died when Black people became more successful. I couldn't conceive that people were still that violently racist and ignorant. Mama explained to me that the KKK was just one example of racism and, as long as there were Black people in this world, racism wouldn't die. I didn't know how to make sense of a world where racism is eternal. Mama explained that there will always be people who won't like me simply because I'm Black. She said, no matter what they told us in school, those days weren't over. The entire time she spoke, the only thing I knew was I never wanted to go to Lexington again. I didn't care how good the barbecue was.

Now, my family had been going to Speedy's Barbecue for the chopped sandwiches for years. To this day, whenever I'm visiting my grandmother, I try to go get her an order of their fresh pork skins at least once. And my first real teaching job was as a sociology instructor at Davidson County Community College. But no matter how many times I went to Speedy's or how many good memories I created in Davidson County to offset that one, I still remembered the day I met the Klan.

The second time came a few short years later, at the start of middle school. Mama enrolled me in Cedar Forest Christian School. In the entire school, I don't think there were ever more than four Black kids at any given time. I can't remember a Black teacher; I can't even remember a Black person working there. While the Black kids came from middle-class families, the White kids were a mix of the superrich and the really poor. I learned this when one of my classmates, whose family owned one of the largest HVAC companies in the city, used the knowledge that another classmate's family received food stamps to win an argument. I was shocked that my other classmate just ran off in embarrassment, because on the south side of Winston-Salem, where I grew up, putting someone's business out like that would have gotten you popped in the mouth. But I was even more shocked at the fact that White people were on welfare. When I told my grandfather this, he told me White people were exactly who government assistance was created for and there were more of them getting checks from the state than Black folk. I carried this little tidbit of knowledge with me and have been side-eyeing White folks' complaints about Black and Brown people on welfare ever since. What unified them, though, was their belief that they were better than Black people.

One day, during free time after lunch, Josh Ashby* asked if I would play basketball with him. If Josh came from money, you couldn't tell. He looked like he didn't bathe and was the type you'd expect to have an entire meth lab in his basement thirty years later. But I didn't have anything else to do so I agreed. Josh asked me to stand underneath the basket first. I assumed we were playing a game of Horse, as we often did, and it wasn't unusual for us to stand close to the basket doing that, so I didn't think anything of it. Within seconds of my standing under the basket, I struggled to catch my breath. I grabbed at whatever was yanking me backward. I heard Josh yell, "Hey, yall! My great-grandpaw said we can hang them just like they did." Able to pull away, I saw that Josh had made a noose out of jump rope and tried to throw the free end into the basketball hoop. My face stung with tears as I looked at my classmates. Some laughed. Some looked away. None of them defended me. Punching Josh in the face didn't erase the pain and humiliation, but it felt good and was well worth the trip to the principal's office.

I hated our principal, Mr. Williams.* He was, without question, an all-around terrible human being. Not only was he racist, but we later learned he was an abusive husband and father. As I sat in his office with tears streaming down my face, he berated me for fighting. He said and did very little to acknowledge how Josh's action had precipitated everything. Instead, he told me if I was so upset by what Josh did, I should have told our teacher and not taken matters into my own hands. I was to be punished. Our school practiced corporal punishment but my mother had not signed the release form allowing it to be used on me and she instructed me to let her know if they ever tried. Mr. Williams told me he'd think of a punishment and let me know before the end of the day. Still crying, I asked to call my mother. He said no. I asked to call my grandmother and he ignored me. I'd just had one of the most horrific experiences of my life and wanted to go home. But I couldn't. I had to go the rest of the day angry, embarrassed, and confused.

By the time Mama picked me up from the after-school program, I was numb. In the car, I didn't say much. Our daily routine was to head to my grandparents' house. There I did my homework, played with my cousins, and ate dinner before we headed back to our side of town. We'd been in the car at least fifteen minutes and were getting on the highway before I told Mama what happened. Before I knew it, she'd done a U-turn on the entry ramp and headed back to the school. When we got there, Mama walked straight into Mr. Williams's office. The secretary didn't even try to stop her; I think she was tired of him, too. I watched my mother light into my principal with the poise and sophistication I'd come to expect from her. Mama didn't have to yell or curse. But she could string together words so eloquent they would cause you to take a minute before you realized you'd just been gutted. I didn't have her finesse and I've never attempted to harness it. Ma didn't raise her voice at Mr. Williams, but she let him know that how he handled this situation was unacceptable. And she made it clear if I ever asked to call her again, I better be given the ability to do so. I watched a man who ruled our Christian school with fear and intimidation cower in front of a Black woman. Mr. Williams apologized profusely to my mother. A few weeks later, I was back in public school.

In the wake of the noose incident, Mama took me to see a therapist. I only attended a few sessions but each was about how the situation at Cedar Forest made me feel. Initially, I could only verbalize that I was embarrassed and it hurt my feelings. It wasn't until later—when fighting for my life in my doctoral program—that I was finally able to say Josh and Mr. Williams taught me a valuable lesson: I couldn't trust White people. Josh had pretended to be my friend and so had the others who stood by and did nothing. And Mr. Williams, denying a traumatized child the opportunity to call her mother, was no better. Ultimately, in therapy, I just flat-out said it. "You can't trust White people. That's why we don't go to church with them. That's why we don't live with them." Looking back, I realize my White therapist had enough reason to ask me to leave her office and never come back but she didn't. And I kept going. "That's why we only deal with them at work and at school. And even there, they can't be trusted. Because, when given the opportunity, they will choose being White every time."

Though Lexington's Klan and my time at Cedar Forest Christian School gave me a crash course in racism, it took longer for me to see the myriad of ways racism functioned in the South, to distinguish where particular White people stood when it came to me, when it came to Black folks. Some White people spoke to you; some acted like they didn't see you. I had teachers who I knew were racist and hated the fact that I was smarter than some of the White kids in the class. They taught me accordingly, though. In the South, the glory days of Dixie still loomed large, and it was no secret some White people missed the days when we knew our place. Hip-hop and continued school integration troubled the waters for many of them. The more their White children and grandchildren were around Black people and consuming our culture, the less hold they had on future generations. And I watched their resentment play out in situations such as being told I wouldn't receive a birthday party invitation like others because a friend's parents or grandparents really didn't like Black people. (I wanted my friends to stand up for me, but we were kids and that was often impossible. I'm less gracious when it happens today.)

In the South, racism is palpable. There's no place you can go where you aren't reminded this was once the stomping ground of racists who are turning over in their graves on account of your freedoms and liberties. The thick, ever-lingering presence of White supremacy makes you adjust your expectations of White people, even as you push them to do better through policy, advocacy, and accountability. And you push them to do better because the Constitution and laws are on your side—not because you actually believe they're going to do the right thing.

Mama made this especially clear to me when I was heading into my first year of seminary. Duke University was my first predominately White educational setting since Cedar Forest. Mama reminded me that the esteemed educational institution wasn't created for students who look like me and, thus, wouldn't care what happened to students who look like me. She told me to "get what you need from them White people and go on about your business." (At some point, I'm sure a lot of Black folks have heard this from their parents or leading Black people and mentors.) She made it clear they had me there to fulfill a quota and to prove they aren't racist. So it was my job to take advantage of resources they made available so I could get ahead. Mama cautioned this is where many educated Black folk get caught up. She said too many of us start to believe what White folks are saying about us—that we're the mythical, magical Negro who's far more capable and accomplished than any they've ever encountered—when it's not true. As I've heard most of my life, nobody lies better than White folk.

I naïvely believed my experiences with Southern racism had prepared me to withstand its Northern iterations. I was wrong. Following graduation from Duke, I headed to New Jersey to begin a doctoral program at one of the leading theological institutions in the country. I was not prepared for how liberal White Christianity and racism would converge.

There had been rumblings about the way the institution treated Black women. Sisters who matriculated there—or attempted to—told stories of gendered oppression at the root of their interactions with faculty, staff, and students. Smart Black women were prey to White academics—their ability to do the work was questioned and gaslit when they sought to bring attention to bias and discrimination. When the administration made me take all my vaccinations over again before I was allowed to officially enroll, I realized there may have been something to the chatter. Confused about why I had to repeat all my shots, one of the administrators joked I could have matriculated through school, since kindergarten, with fake medical records. When he and the other administrator saw my stone face did not change, they stopped laughing. When I vented to Mama, she reminded me that the higher and deeper into the ranks of the academy I sought to go, the more I would encounter White people who didn't want me there. According to her, this would not be the last such encounter.

I bit my tongue at the new-student reception when I met a doctoral student just finishing comprehensive exams who had heard about my desired research project—exploring the theological implications of mass incarceration—and told me they wished they could do a "niche project" like mine. What I was doing would really help people, they said, and it was frustrating that they couldn't pursue their passion too; rather they had to focus on theology proper and write for the masses. These White people were different and would take some getting used to.

Although I completed my French language requirement during the summer session, classes didn't officially begin until after Labor Day. Mama died two months later. To say I was in a fog would have been an understatement. Through my adviser, a liberal White man beloved in the field, I asked for a leave of absence. It was denied. I asked for a leave of absence three times, and each time it was denied. Sympathetic and advocating for me, my adviser told me the administrators couldn't figure out how to allow me to stay in my campus apartment while on a semester leave so they decided it was easier to say no. When I explained to him the difficulty of concentrating on work, he assured me he was relaying all of this to them. I kept his emails and correspondence where he explained to me that the institution just didn't get it. One administrator even went as far as to say she didn't understand why I was still requesting a leave of absence six months after my mother died. According to her, I should've adjusted by then.

But I hadn't adjusted. I couldn't breathe. The loss of my mother was suffocating, and knowing she'd been only two months away from defending her own doctoral dissertation made attempting to complete my coursework impossible. I just needed a moment. I needed time. Not to read a book, write a paper, or participate in class discussion. I needed a moment to just breathe and be. I needed room to fall apart and cry without having to hold it together for a three-hour doctoral seminar.

Instead, every administrator I met with reminded me that taking care of myself wasn't why I was there. They went on at length about the honor of being accepted into the PhD program. One went as far as to tell me how many others applied the year I did. Asking for a leave of absence, even after they told me no, made me "ungrateful." One administrator actually used that word. To them, I was a mule; nothing mattered more than the work I was brought there to produce. I was supposed to be like my ancestors who watched their loved ones die, be killed, or be sold off, and had no choice but to keep working in the fields while they mourned.

So I went through the motions—a shell of myself in a classroom, a shred of myself in a paper. I vented to close friends about the constant denial of my requests for time and leaned on them as they helped me keep my head above water, sometimes even reading books for me and giving me notes so I could just rest. Things came to a head when, after experiencing sexual assault in my campus apartment, I asked to be moved to another one. There were vacant apartments in my building, and I would, of course, assume the cost of the move. When I met with the director of housing and the seminary president, my request was declined. The president did tell me he'd keep me in his prayers, though.

Months later, I received a two-page letter stating the administration was not confident in my ability to proceed in the program and a vote to dismiss me was being entertained. I had the opportunity to appeal and I did, providing a fifty-page counterargument, which included emails from my adviser citing the institution's negligence. But, in the heat of the fire, my adviser ultimately apologized to the administration for misspelled and omitted words in his emails to me that could've suggested the institution was at fault in any way. And in the vote hearing, this White man—who taught feminist and womanist theology courses—threw a Black woman under the bus to save himself.

Faced with the weight of my counterargument, my institution gave me one more chance to request a leave of absence. I refused. I'd asked three times and, each time, I was denied. Nothing had changed now other than the fact that they saw I had receipts. If they were going to give me a leave of absence, they could go back and retroactively grant one of the three I'd already requested. I wasn't asking again. I wasn't about to beg White people to see me as human and do what even they knew they should've done. I refused to submit another request and they voted to dismiss me.

A few days after I'd been told I was dismissed, the same administrator who called me ungrateful for requesting a leave of absence offered me five thousand dollars if I went away quietly. He said the five thousand dollars was a gesture of goodwill so I wouldn't be "homeless" and I was lucky to be getting that. Until then, the gall of White people didn't amaze me. Even if they didn't have much, they rarely lacked the audacity. I reached out to an attorney who guided me through the process of filing a complaint with the Department of Education about how my civil rights had been violated. When confronted with their negligence, the institution opted to settle. I took the money, which was substantially more than the five thousand dollars hush money, and started a new life—one that would not include pursuing a PhD or being a part of theological education ever again.

My experiences with White people taught me that being Black, to them, was a crime. How dare my mother and I be Black and move through the streets of Lexington of our own accord? How dare I attend a private school with White children and think I was equal to them? And how dare I demand an institution founded by slaveholders, where slave quarters are still used as dormitories, treat me humanely in the wake of my mother's passing and after experiencing sexual assault? And these White people claim to love Jesus.

Even as a kid, I was amazed by how we had weekly chapel

services at Cedar Forest and the Holy Ghost didn't convict Josh, Mr. Williams, and the rest of the White supremacists there—young and old—to be better people. Sunday services never pricked the hearts of those Klansmen in Lexington, and it didn't matter that my doctoral program professors and administrators taught and wrote about Jesus; they clearly didn't know him. They believed in a White God and believed their White skin was holy and endowed them with the power to wreak havoc in the lives of anybody who didn't look like them. Nothing changed their minds. They could never meet enough "good" Black people for them to interrogate their beliefs. They were racist and ignorant, exactly who they wanted to be.

And then, there were the well-meaning White people— who heard about my experiences and the experiences of others and wanted me to know they were not like "them," the Whites who had treated me so bad. They were different. They didn't see race. When they saw me, they didn't see a Black girl or a Black woman. They saw a human being. They didn't understand why that wasn't a compliment to me. When I had the energy, I let them know I shouldn't have to be rendered colorless and have my entire identity dismissed to be seen as human. And often, they just dismissed me as being too angry or emotional and said they would pray for me. Other times, I was too exhausted by those "good" White people who couldn't understand how not seeing color was just as dangerous as their cousins' intention to harm me *because* of my color. White Christians I encountered at Duke Divinity were the best at this, though. They loved to tell us this was their first time confronting their Whiteness and we needed to give them grace and space. They found a few Black folks to coddle them in their foolishness. I, on the other hand, wasn't having it.

I grew up in a faith context which affirmed my Blackness. Yes, church had its issues, but it certainly let me know it is okay to be Black. And my church affirmed Jesus is Blackity Black. My pastors, Sunday School teachers, and youth leaders reminded us God made us Black. If we were supposed to be anything else, God would have ensured it. My mother also placed me in community youth programs and initiatives where Black was lifted up as beautiful. Our heritage, our culture, and our potential were our greatest strengths. I grew up believing I could do anything because I was Black, not in spite of it.

Yet, while these messages concerning the power and wonder of Black people were unanimous, approaches to racism were contradictory. In the church, I was taught civil disobedience and taking the higher road was the best route. If a White person was spewing racism and bigotry, you don't throw it back at them. Instead, you turn the other cheek and watch God use your integrity to elevate you over them. The community programs gave us a different approach. They told us we should defend ourselves at all cost. We had as much right to check a White person for talking crazy as they thought they had to say what they did. These polarized viewpoints embodied the divide between how the Black Church understood the fight against racism and how institutions detached from religious affiliation did. I opted for the confrontational approach. If you said something to me, I was always going to say something back. I hadn't met a White person I feared too much to tell how I felt.

I also blame my grandmother. When I was a child, Grandma told me not to be afraid of any White person or believe they were better than me. "They put their underwear on one leg at a time just like you do," she said. "Now, the day you find one who puts their drawers on top of their head and they end up on the same way as yours, then that's one White person worth listening to." As a child, I recited this advice often. Mama would joke how Grandma made me more of a rebel than either of them probably would've liked. Sometimes, I think they're right.

I don't have a problem telling White people what I think about them. Sheleda often reminds me how I went off on a White police officer who was less than helpful after we'd been victims of a hit-and-run at a Walmart while in college. And I understand how dangerous going toe-to-toe with the officer was and how privileged it is to say whatever I've got to say to White folk. Too many Black folks lost their lives and freedom standing up for honorable reasons. I respect that and understand why, when dealing with White people, others may feel the need to take a different, what they consider to be safer, approach. But I also understand there are no circumstances under which White supremacy will see us as human and not try to kill us. And if we know this, then why not be exactly who we want to be? More important, why not be who God created us to be? God made me Black. It is how God decided I would show up in the world. Black womanhood is the lens through which I see the world and am seen. There is absolutely nothing wrong with that. There is nothing wrong with me being Black. The problem is only in when I am mistreated for being so.

But not everyone was brought up the same way I was. It wasn't until I got to seminary that I encountered millennial Black Christians who weren't raised in the traditional Black Church context. And I don't mean they were Methodists, Episcopalians, or other mainline denominations. I didn't know there were Black people who *chose* to go to church with White people. That made absolutely no sense to me. Church was sacred space, the only place we could get away from White people. Why would Black people want to be there with them? I didn't even think Black and White folk worshipped the same Jesus, to be honest. White people have long associated their status and position in society with God's blessings and providence. When we're in church, we're not only asking God to deliver us from our personal trials, we're also asking God to deliver us from the shit White people do to us. I mean, I know a lot of Black Christians who don't even think White people are going to Heaven!

It was hard for me to understand Black people who drank White folks' Kool-Aid when it came to Christianity. And I don't understand the ones who are still drinking it but have found cooler, more benevolent ways to say the same things. I reject folks who tell us we must surrender our ethnic and cultural identities to Jesus. It's the new evangelical way to sidestep accountability for sowing and watering anti-Black seeds across Christendom. These responses to the waves of unjust killings of Black and Brown people, telling us to "just surrender who we are to Jesus," sound cute if you don't know what they're saying. Essentially, these answers to heightened racism are thinly veiled attempts to suggest if marginalized people were more like Jesus (read: White), they wouldn't be killed. And to complete the smoke screen, they'll have one of their non-White evangelical darlings standing in front of crowds of White people exclaiming how they would be vengeful and full of hatred in their hearts at Whites had they not given themselves and their identities over to Jesus. And folks eat it up, too.

The same God who wrapped Godself in Brown skin to be brought into the world also made me. I don't have to surrender an identity God has already deemed sacred. And I'm certainly not using my identity to create a false sense of superiority and domination. If *anyone* should give their identities over to the Divine, it is definitely White people. What would this world be if the daily prayer of White people was to be made less *White*? To be decentered and made to honor the lived experiences of others? What would White people do if they realized God intended for their culture and experiences to be expressed equally alongside those of the rest of humanity? Can they hurry up and figure it out?

Every day, I wake up grateful to be Black. And then, I go on social media and look at the trending hashtags and conversations of humor and hope, created by Black Twitter, and it reminds me how we, as a people, are undefeated. And even in social and digital spaces, it's clear how the culture vultures want everything but the burden. I don't know how many times I've chuckled at a White person's tweet, heavy with our cultural idioms, or a picture where they've clearly ripped off our aesthetic being quote-tweeted with the poignant question: Why are you in Black people's business?

Blackness is a gift and blessing. The burden attached to Blackness isn't mine, though. It is the sin and shame White people carry for denying our divinity. And I get it. If I'd spent centuries trying to make myself synonymous with God, I would deeply resent the existence of the very ones who prove me to be a lie. That's why I am honored Black is the way God wanted to present me to the world. Those Lexington Klansmen, Josh and Mr. Williams, and those Christian racists at my doctoral program couldn't take that away from me. Nobody can.*

---

* *These names have been changed because I'm not about to pay a bigot any of my hard-earned money.*

AMAZING GRACE FOR
SIDE CHICKS

Mama was silent for what felt like an eternity after I told her. When she started speaking, I almost wished she hadn't. "Candice, I don't know what's dumber. You telling me you're involved with a married man or you believing that he's going to do right by you." I'd just told my mother that for the last four years, I'd been having an affair. I understood her frustration—she couldn't believe I'd gotten myself into this. But why couldn't she see this was different? He wasn't some lowlife sneaking around on his wife. It actually just happened; we didn't mean to fall in love and did everything we could to fight it. He was my best friend. This wasn't some casual hookup off a dating app. We actually loved each other.

Plus, he was a good man. Fresh off receiving his license to preach and getting a job on the church staff, he told the story of how his former boss told him he couldn't casually date women. Because of his role as a preacher, he'd have to date for marriage and be committed to the relationship. And he did.

He met and married the first woman he dated in the church, following his pastor's directions. Ironically, a cheating scandal and divorce were right around the corner for the senior pastor, though, proving my lover's boss was more of the "do as I say . . . not as I do" type of leader. Nevertheless, he wasn't going to divorce her and break up the home they'd created for their two children. He remembered what his parents' divorce (and then their remarriage to each other) did to him. He couldn't stand his father because of it and didn't want the same fate for him and his son. The daughter of a trifling daddy, I understood and respected his decision. He was a dedicated father, even if his devotion meant sacrificing his own happiness.

On some level, it didn't matter, because we were really friends first. Even though romance evolved rather quickly, we had been in each other's orbits for a long time. Writing for the same online Black progressive Christian publication and having many of the same friends and colleagues, we knew *of* each other before we knew each other. By the time we connected, we respected one another first—respected each other's talent, each other's minds. We talked about current events and theology often, me pushing him in places where he was progressive in theory but not in practice and him pushing me where my expectations of others were slightly unrealistic. We'd even seriously considered presenting together when our academic guilds were hosting an annual conference in Baltimore and made a religious and theological exploration of HBO's *The Wire* their special theme. Our presentation would've imagined a sixth season of the acclaimed show and explicitly explored the role of the Black Church in addressing and perpetuating social decline in urban areas. For some reason, our collaboration didn't happen, and I was silently grateful it didn't. Our relationship had not yet become physical, and, in the throes of the postacademic-presentation high, we would've had a hard time avoiding taking it there.

In the beginning, I did my best not to allow our relationship to cross the line—no matter how blurry that line had been. We were in constant communication for chunks of the day. We'd even started calling each other by pet names. He was my Tea Cake. I confessed to him I reread *Their Eyes Were Watching God* annually and I found myself resonating with Janie when it came to him. Everything about falling for him made no sense, so I tried not to; I honestly did. I told him I was going to fast from him for the entire Lenten season. He smirked and nodded his head. "Okay," he said. He didn't push me. On some level, I believed he understood how difficult it was not to lean into this because he was feeling the same things I was. Over Google video chat, I stared at the most beautiful man I'd ever seen. His eyes and his smile melted me, but I knew, if I could just get through these forty days and forty nights, we could right the ship and become real friends again. I don't think my fast lasted three days.

I tried to explain to Mama that, even though things were murky, we really loved and respected each other. She wasn't having it. No matter how much I explained his situation and overemphasized his positive attributes, all that mattered to my mother was he was still someone else's husband and she was thoroughly disappointed in me.

Telling my mother I was a side chick wasn't necessarily the

best decision I'd ever made. It was worse than the time I was in college and called to tell her my then-boyfriend had cheated on me, while I slipped in I'd had sex for the first time. Mama could barely understand what I was saying through my tears. She told me when I became a mother, I'd understand the helplessness of being hours away from your distressed child and feeling unable to do anything about her pain. That night, I confessed to her I was no longer a virgin. I'd snuck back into the state to have sex for the first time in a Country Inn & Suites in Raleigh, and the boy (whom she loathed) was cheating on me with another college freshman at NC A&T. After I spilled my heart to her, Mama told me everything would be okay. She prayed with me, told me there was nothing I could do to make her love me any less, and told me to get some sleep. At nineteen, I went to bed feeling like this mistake wasn't unto death because my mama had my back. I would need my rest because Mama woke me up at 6:00 the next morning to go slam off on me for being so ridiculous and sneaky.

With this confession, however, Mama's reaction was much different—she didn't speak to me with empathy for my nineteen-year-old broken heart. She talked to me like I was a grown woman who'd made a very dangerous bed. And though a part of me regretted telling her, I was in love. I mean *head-over-heels, I completely understood why no other relationship worked because we were meant for each other* in love. The kind of love I didn't want to have to lie about if she asked me. I was spending so many hours of the day in communication with him I thought it inevitable for her to ask why I was always on my phone or rushed to my computer. I hated hiding things from her. Even if it meant her cocking her head to the side and arching those eyebrows all the way into her forehead before she went into a monologue that would definitely make me feel stupid about my choices, I felt better after she knew.

He didn't tell anyone and, of course, I understood why. Once, I cried and told him, if something happened to me, Sheleda knew to get in touch with him, even though she was adamantly opposed to the relationship. But, otherwise, if something happened to him, I would have to find out through the grapevine or on social media. To appease me, he told me he'd instructed his brother to get in touch with me should anything ever happen to him. We laughed as he told me he referred to me as his "bestie" and his brother asked what grown-ass man has one of those.

"So where do you see this going?" Ma sounded exasperated. I pretended I didn't understand the question, so she repeated it. I knew what I wanted. I wanted him. I wanted a family. I wanted what he said I gave him: life. I wanted to be loved by him proudly in the light of day.

But to say such out loud sounded crazy. *Maybe Mama was right.* So after all the truth telling, I told her a lie. "I just want us to be friends." And she knew it was a lie.

Ma said I wouldn't have told her if I didn't want it to become something more. I was about to move closer to him to begin doctoral studies and I didn't know what would ensue, being in closer proximity. "You want a life with him but that's not going to happen. Not this way. You can't build your happiness on someone else's misery, Candice. You can't."

Throughout my life, I'd heard my mother say those words

to other people but I didn't think she'd ever say them to me. Neither did she. Mama got up from the dining room table and walked past me with a posture informing me she'd never been more disappointed in me than she was right then. I'd heard, "You don't have to buy the cow if the milk is free" or "If they'll cheat with you, they'll cheat on you." I knew Mama was trying to prevent the destruction she saw coming, but it wasn't coming and, somehow, I'd have to get her to see this was different. Months later, she would be dead and he'd be the second phone call I made after I found out.

Before Mama died, this man had grown distant in ways uncharacteristic of our time together. We'd gone from talking several times a day to almost nothing. I didn't know what was going on with him and, when Mama died, I didn't have the energy to find out. He did his best to be there for me. With a house full of people, I sat in my mother's garage on the phone with him as he helped me craft what I would say at her funeral. He apologized profusely for the fact he wouldn't be there. Now a senior pastor himself, he had to eulogize one of his deacons the same day. While I completely understood, I was heartbroken. My friends had come from across the country to be with me as I buried my mom and I wanted him to be there, too. But I knew that even if there was no deacon to lay to rest, he still couldn't have been there for me in the ways I needed. Mama passed on November 14, 2015. I stayed in North Carolina until January 1, 2016. A few days after returning to New Jersey, I met him at the Dave & Buster's in Pelham, New York, and he told me he was getting a divorce.

I sat there stunned as he explained that his distance from

me was his way of navigating the reality that his marriage was ending. I'd assumed she'd somehow found out about us and he didn't want to tell me while I was dealing with Mama. But when he told me she hadn't and he was the one filing the papers, I asked him one question. "Did I do this?"

For years, I'd been loving him in secret but the idea that I could have been the reason this was happening brought instant shame and regret. It was a foolish feeling, quite incongruent with the truth of how I felt for him, but it was the truth. As we spent the next few hours playing videogames, with him beating me in arcade basketball, I slowly began to believe him and lean into the possibility, after all these years, we could finally be together.

Ten months later, in October, he stood in his apartment filled with furniture from my mother's home and told me he didn't want to be with me anymore. He said he only saw us as friends. Sure, we'd crossed some boundaries but, he said, ultimately, he never saw me as anything more than a really good friend. We'd still communicate and sleep with each other in what I thought were attempts to stumble toward a happily ever after. We'd spend my birthday together and even exchange Christmas gifts that year. We'd make love a final time in January 2017, where he held me in his bed as I cried and he assured me he wasn't dating anyone else. But, in December 2017, he'd be married to wife number two. And I'd learn he'd married someone else from the anonymous email sent to my blog address, titled "Happy New Year" and filled with pictures from his wedding.

Something—now I know it was Spirit not wanting me to

be alone—urged me to buy a plane ticket and ring in the new year with Sheleda and her family. She met me in baggage claim, right after I turned on my phone and read the email. And we did what we always do when a boy breaks my heart. We headed straight to the mall for some ice cream and retail therapy.

By the time I was sent candids from his wedding, I'd become numb to receiving pictures anonymously. After I made him get rid of my mother's furniture, the picture of his new furniture was definitely sent to drive home the message I'd done nothing to break their stride. The one of him asleep in bed was especially cruel but not as harsh as the ones of their family vacations where they took the kids to what looked to be Disney. Perhaps the most painful picture was the one *he* sent of my mother's furniture thrown on the back of a junk-hauling truck, the Saturday before Mother's Day of that year. I'd told him there was no way he could keep my mother's things while beginning a relationship with someone else. That was a level of disrespect even he should not have cared to explore. I was angry, so I gave him a deadline to donate my mother's furniture to charity or I'd report it stolen. I knew there was no actual way I could say he stole it. I just wanted him to hurt like he'd hurt me. But when he emailed me that picture of pieces of her furniture in a truck and wrote "Don't ever contact me again," I knew there was absolutely no way I could hurt him as much as he hurt me. To make things worse, the motto on the truck was "We get rid of the junk you don't want."

Although he sent me the junk truck pictures, he denied he

and his wife were behind any of the other emails and pictures I'd received through my blog. But I didn't believe him; they were too personal to be sent by anyone else. My friends would try to reassure me I'd dodged a bullet—that he wasn't who I thought he was and I should be grateful our lives weren't further intertwined, but it was hard to believe that. I was fielding so many questions in my head. I didn't understand what I'd done to deserve this specific kind of evil. He'd moved on. There was no need to rub salt in the wound. When I would ask myself what I did to merit this torture, I could only surmise it was because I loved him. From January 2016 to December 2017, this man I'd loved from the depths of my soul became unrecognizable. He became my enemy.

When it came to the painful stuff, I didn't have an "I told you so" Mama. She was too empathetic for cruelty. If anything, she would've held me as my world completely unraveled. I was humiliated. Nothing I'd thought was true about my relationship with him actually was. It wasn't *only* me—there were *three* others *in addition to me*. We attended our guilds' annual conference in San Diego the year before my mother died. After making love, he wanted to rush back to a session to see one of his friends present. I was livid; he knew we had very little time to be together. I pointedly asked him if anything was going on between the two of them. He kissed me and told me he was just going to support a friend. When she and I finally talked, we learned how our time lines with him overlapped. He'd even taken what I'd shared with him about *Their Eyes Were Watching God* and started calling her *his* Janie. He'd been sending her flowers, too. Finding chunks of time to emphasize his devotion to her, too. Telling her he wanted to be with her, too. She was smarter than me, though. She told me they didn't sleep together. According to her, that's how they could remain friends when he and I had become adversaries.

The more the truth came out about him, the clearer it became Mama was right all along, and it broke my heart I wouldn't be able to ask how she knew. She hadn't met him but she knew he'd been lying from the beginning of our time together. How? Was it from personal experience or second-hand knowledge? And, honestly, these weren't appropriate questions to ask her. If she'd wanted me to know what convinced her I'd end up here, she would have told me. But you also don't ask those questions because no one willingly admits to being caught up in an affair. Correction: most *women* don't go around talking about this. Plenty of men have friends who will hold the secrets of their affairs, co-conspiring with alibis and creative lies. But women, especially sisters trying to do right, don't have many spaces for that kind of cosign. Only a small handful of my girls knew about our relationship and they weren't happy about it. They thought more of me than they felt I did, and I couldn't get them to see that this was a small hurdle on the road to happiness with this man. Imagine believing a whole marriage is a small and insignificant disruption to your fairy tale.

People get into affairs for a number of reasons. Some say it's just for the sex. Others fall in love, like I did. I've met people who are strategic about their dalliances. They get in and they get out. That wasn't me. So many lines were blurred and, whenever I prayed for strength, I interpreted his reinvested interest and commitment to make me happy as signs to stay. We call it "struggle love," the belief that women have to go through shit to get to sunshine. And this belief is easily upheld in worlds where we see men get what they want, at everyone else's expense. If you're a woman and you want to be happy with a man, it's understood you're going to have many a sleepless night. It's expected, at some point, he's going to make you look like a fool. But if you're lucky, you and your foolish self will get chosen by him. And you and the children will live in the wonderful house he provides, go on the vacations his money pays for, and all of the moments in between will help to wash the clown makeup off your face. I believed my guilt about our affair and my tearful nights spent alone were the seeds I was sowing for my harvest. And though many of those crops would be spoiled (you reap what you sow, right?), my harvest would be sharing his last name, a child made from our love and life together.

You can't be a side chick and expect to be treated well. I don't mean the gifts and trips. I got those. Being flown to whatever conference he was attending, I stayed in the room or made sure to keep a low profile while he attended his sessions. And it took me months to throw away the two sets of pearl earrings from Tiffany & Co. he got me for my birthday and "just because." The *Game of Thrones* book set he sent, after I binged the show to catch up with him, got tossed as soon as I learned he used a variation of the show's name for his wedding hashtag. Supporting my academic and theological pursuits, he bought so many of the books I mentioned to him in casual conversation. When I threw away the ESV translation of the bible he'd bought me, I asked God to forgive me and understand why I couldn't give a bible, purchased by the devil, to anyone else. And I got my fair share of attention. In fact, at times, it honestly didn't make sense we weren't together. We'd had so many late-night conversations from his attic when he was supposed to be reading for his doctoral program. I knew I would wake up every Sunday morning to an email with his sermon manuscript attached. When I would get frustrated and ask why we just couldn't be together, we'd both cry and remember the commitment he'd made to his family.

So I'm not talking about the tangible things. What I mean is you can't be in an affair and expect to be treated ethically. I was actively participating in this man being dishonest to his wife, the mother of his children, and was expecting him to be honest with me, simply because I was honest with him. I told him about every guy and thought my honesty was being reciprocated. It would take years for me to understand, even if love and care are present, a structure built on lies will be faulty. And, no matter how much we love them, we know better.

We *know* better. Any person who finds themselves in this position, and has a conscience, has this on a loop in their heads. I had it on a loop in mine. I would negotiate parts of my conscience away to justify staying, and no justification was greater than the reality that I loved him and he loved me. Our love kept me with him when he explained why it wouldn't be a good idea for me to attend his first pastoral installation, even if other friends were there to create a foil. Our love kept me there when two kids became three and he told me one Sunday morning before service because he didn't want me to see a congratulatory post on social media. Our love made me track down his college basketball coach at the 2016 Olympic Games in Rio to get his college jersey so I could give it to him as a gift when he was installed as pastor at his next church—an installation, thanks to his separation and pending divorce, I *was* able to attend. That abundant and unconditional love was what made me understand why it was trickier for him to publicly show up for me in the ways that mattered. We believe what we want to believe when we don't want to admit the truth. Deep down, I knew this was wrong, but my hope, and my belief in him, was palpable. It was there.

I believed him. I believed absolutely everything he ever said to me. I believed him in January 2017, when he told me there was no one else. When I showed up at his church three months later, for his all-clergywomen "Seven Last Words" Good Friday service and saw her sitting alone in the second row, it was the first time I had to confront the reality that not only had he been lying to me, but also he'd moved on. The service was over and I couldn't chance going into his office to get the pink lemonade layer cake and card I had placed on his desk. Someone would definitely see me, and I didn't have enough strength to walk to his office and my car without completely falling apart. It was as if the last part of my heart not crushed by my mother's death was obliterated. It was soul pain, the kind so deep you can't even cry. Maybe it was arrogance on my part or maybe it was sheer naïveté but I never thought he'd do anything like that to me. It was true: if they'll use you to hurt someone else, they won't think twice about hurting you.

And, if you're a woman, you'll be surrounded by messages saying you deserved it. Everywhere we go, there's something to remind us that mistresses are the scourge of the Earth. People can have empathy for a woman falling victim to a man's shenanigans but, as soon as they find out she was "the other woman," compassion goes out the window. "That's what she gets." On some level, it makes sense. Affairs do more than wreck marriages; they break spirits and wound souls. What kind of woman would do that?

Apparently, when we're born, we're encoded with a solidarity with other women. If sisters can't find honor or respect among the men in their lives—men who are expected to cheat, if we're honest—we should be able to get it from each other. And we do. When men's nonsense breaks our hearts, we find refuge in our sisters. And this is why we don't have many friends who will justify our affairs. What do we look like asking for empathy from women who came to us torn apart after learning their husbands' secrets?

Be clear: being a mistress automatically revokes your feminist card. I've had to work to earn mine back. It's pretty hard to say you advocate for the rights of women when, in your personal life, you're actively destroying a woman.

We love the story of the woman caught in the act of adultery because we get Jesus's famous words in John 8:7, "let he who is without sin cast the first stone." Yet, no matter how much folks may quote this scripture, the world isn't any easier for women still caught up in these kinds of situations. But who asks the woman *how* she got there? What did he say to her? What did she believe? Why did she believe it? There's a story behind the woman and the man and that story matters. It's only with the story that she, and the rest of us, can finally get to the truth.

While I was angry at and humiliated by his lies, I had no excuse to avoid confronting the parts of myself that got me into this mess and doing the work to transform. I want to say I came to this conclusion on my own but I didn't. I had already been in counseling to come to terms with my mother's passing, and when things shifted in our relationship, it took me to an even darker place. The compounded grief around Mama's death, the extreme shame I had about giving some of my mother's things to him, and the pain of his betrayal were suffocating, and if I was going to live, I would have to address it. This was literally a matter of life and death. So, no matter how much *he* lied, I had to tell the truth. I had to be honest and admit our relationship was rooted in my feelings of insufficiency. On some level, I believed the pain of secrecy was the price to pay for the right to public love. My unresolved stuff about my father and my deep insecurities showed up and made it so easy for me to accept these fragments of love and convince myself the love was whole.

But no matter how much therapy work I was doing, I was still broken and angry. People tell women not to be bitter and jaded, but those are human emotions. I had every right to feel them, whether or not I'd "put" myself in this position. By no means was I making myself a victim but it angered me the ways I had to carry the shame of this relationship alone. He was able to create a narrative supporting what he knew was a lie. While he was rewarded with pastoral anniversaries, wedding and baby showers, and the adoration of his academic and preaching colleagues, I endured the whispers and rumors. It was easier for folks not to believe me in a world that tends *not* to believe women—especially ones who sleep with married men.

When Jesus told the woman's accusers to throw their rocks if they were sinless, they dropped them and walked away. When Jesus asked where her accusers had gone, it's as if he hoped those of us in similar circumstances could realize we aren't inferior to women who haven't been in affairs. They are not better than we are because their brokenness didn't lead them into the arms of another woman's husband. To tell the truth, it's quite possible a woman's brokenness is what led her to marry and stay with that man. I see this with more than a few couples who try to convince us they are #relationshipgoals on social media. We are all broken in some way or another. Our responsibility is to identify and heal it.

It's Jesus's command to "go and sin no more" that reminds us we have the capacity to be better than who we have been. I've had many conversations about whether "love" can be a sin; I don't think so. The sin Jesus asked the woman caught in adultery to abandon is whatever enabled her to believe and act differently than what she now knew to be true: she was worthy of full, whole, and complete love. When we've healed those parts of us, we can't go back and do as we did before. It doesn't mean couples who start out as cheating partners can't make it. It does, however, mean real truth-telling, and the work to repair what has been destroyed has to happen in order to reset the relationship on a solid foundation. I'm happy to say I have my feminist card back. In public and in private, I live into my allegiance to women and the world I want to see. I want a world where women are not stoned, literally and figuratively, for our mistakes. I also want a world where women don't experience the pain that leads to certain mistakes. I can't stop all the pain but I can do my part.

The idea that we can do these things and have the capacity to change is the grace of God. We've spent our entire lives thanking God for it. For giving us the very thing we can never earn and do not deserve. If given the choice between receiving grace and reaping what I have sown, I'll take grace every time.

Grace doesn't blind us to who we have been—or shield us from taking accountability for the pain we cause—but it provides us with second, third, fourth, and hundredth chances to become better people. Grace comes with a reminder God didn't leave us where God found us but extended the opportunity to learn and unlearn behaviors for a better next time. Grace empowered me to confront what I'd intentionally ignored. Grace shows up in all of us asking the hard questions to break new ground.

Grace is generous and, when we lean into it, we can't help but extend it to others. The lens of grace enabled me to recognize the brokenness of others even when they didn't see it themselves. Admittedly, I have wondered about him. I wonder if he has finally admitted the lies he told others and the ones he told himself. I wonder if he's healed the parts that led him to relationships outside his first marriage and led him to believe he had the right to leave disaster in his wake. I hope he's intentioned to become the good man he pretended to be for so many years. But that kind of growth and transformation takes real risk. Unfortunately so many of us have mastered the art of superficial evolution; going beyond the surface to really be our best selves jeopardizes everything we've worked so hard for. When it comes to me, doing the hard work of digging things up from the root is far better than just cutting the grass.

I am light-years from the woman I was during our time together but celebrating my growth isn't constant. There are days I look back and cringe at how lost and broken I was. And there are days when I look back and smile at how far I have come. A full life is one filled with mistakes. Mama was right. Getting involved with him was dumb, and the depth of the pain I experienced rearranged my soul. Even as I heal, I'm still fighting against the residue. Perhaps there are parts I'll always be reeling from. We were not meant to experience or cause this much pain. Sometimes, our mistakes harm more than just ourselves. The weight and responsibility of what we've done is ours and ours alone to bear. And, in bearing it, we hope for an opportunity to transform—made possible because we serve a God who believes we can. That belief in us should be enough for us to at least try.

WE SHOULD ALL BE
WOMANISTS

I always wanted a sister. Whether she was older or younger, I wanted a built-in best friend and keeper of my secrets. Envious of the sister relationships I knew, I wished Mama would have adopted or had another girl. And it wasn't like I didn't know that things between sisters could be complicated. I had Mama's own relationships with her two sisters as proof. The middle of three girls, Mama was much closer to her younger sister, Aunt Darlene, than to her older sister. The last fifteen years of my aunt Darlene's life, she and Mama were inseparable. For our monthly family movie trips, Mama was always late. Aunt Darlene never complained but she made it clear she liked seeing the movie previews and didn't want to sit in the front rows because the good seats were gone by the time they arrived. Mama and Aunt Darlene laughed and giggled with each other on our annual vacations to Myrtle Beach. The last year of Aunt Darlene's life, Mama kept calling her "the best baby sister in the world," and my aunt would look at her, smile, and say, "my Debbie." I wanted what they had.

My older aunt, on the other hand, taught me that not every sister is your friend and some people are connected to you only by blood—not by ethics, care, or real kinship.

Still, as an only child, I wanted one or more sisters. I was convinced, even if we were different, we would still be close because Mama would've raised us that way. And I found mine—even if not connected by sharing a womb. Growing up with a family of cousins, I'm still tight with my younger cousin Dominique. She's the one closest to my age and, before she got her own sister, we were raised like sisters. My amazing older godsisters, Tonja and Trevette, love me like I *am* their own flesh and blood. My homegirls from college became the sisters I prayed for and, when I was initiated into Alpha Kappa Alpha, I got more sisters than I would ever know what to do with. I may have been an only child in theory but I was a younger *and* older sister at the same time.

Through her friendships, Mama showed me how to make sisters. There's Aunt Porscha, her best friend from college, whom she met in the registration line in 1974. There's Aunt Doris and Aunt Clara, Mama's best friends from church. There's Aunt Jan, Mama's best friend from work. Basically, my mother's friends were my "aunts." I was taught to put a handle on the names of women who are beloved, a handle speaking to the depths of the relationship and respect. My mother's relationships with these women became the blueprint for moving friendships beyond the boundaries and becoming family. Because they *were* our family. They were the family we got to create. I ended up with aunts, uncles, and cousins as close as—and even closer than—my own kin, and it didn't require my mother being married into my father's family or anyone else's. All she had to do was be a good friend.

During the week before Mama's funeral, people came to tell stories of her care and kindness. Some of those stories I knew; others I didn't. That's how Mama liked it. She couldn't stand folks helping people then "showboating," as she called it. "If you're in a position to help somebody, then you help them. But what you did is between you, them, and your God. The world don't need to know." She absolutely hated when people would do some charitable act, as a group or individually, then post it on social media. She laid me out when she saw me do it and I didn't do it again.

One story moved everyone who heard it, including me. Another "aunt," one of my mother's friends from her days working at Baptist Hospital, asked if I remembered the morning I woke to find her on our couch. I lied and told her I vaguely remembered it. I didn't want to tell her that not only did I remember that morning, I remembered the night before, when she banged on our door. Mama let her in. I couldn't hear much from my room but she was crying and slightly hysterical. Mama calmed her down. When Ma came to check on me and close my bedroom door, I pretended to be asleep.

My aunt went on to fill in the blanks. Her husband had been abusive and she just couldn't take it anymore. She ran to the one place she felt she could be safe: our home. Not only would she be safe, but no one would know she was there. Mama instructed me not to tell anyone, including my grandma and granddaddy, she was staying with us. I didn't. My aunt would go on to tell us how she'd go back to my uncle and it would be years before she finally left him for good. But Mama didn't abandon her, giving her money for hotels and letting her stay in our apartment when I was in school. My aunt told us that many nights when Ma worked third shift and I spent the night with my grandparents, she was at our house. She was safe. My mother would be there when she filed for divorce, leaving the marriage with all she could carry. More important, when other women in her life, family included, would tell my uncle where she was, my mother didn't. My aunt said Mama helped her trust women again. She couldn't say all Black women were bad because she knew a really good one.

When I'd ask Mama what makes a good friend, she'd say, "Jesus." He was her answer for everything. I know my mother's commitment to being a great friend was rooted in her commitment to being a good Christian but there was so much more. Not all my "aunts" were Christian, and the ones who were, varied in their levels of devotion and participation. And yet their love and devotion for each other was unwavering. There was more to the reason my mama and her friends modeled true sisterhood with each other.

I was first introduced to the concept of womanism, a framework created by Alice Walker, as an undergrad at Tennessee State in the Black Woman course offered in Africana Studies. In that class, we were taught the difference between Black feminism and womanism. My friends and I still really couldn't distill it then but something felt distant about womanism. We would joke that Black feminism was for everybody and womanism was for Black women who had money, which is to say womanism felt a little elitist and out of touch for most of us. Time in seminary would change my understanding of womanism altogether.

I went to Duke with a number of questions, born out of my work as a sociologist and out of the death of Whitney. I was trying to understand the realities of Black theology for Black girls like me. There were plenty of books and papers about Black women from Mama's and previous generations, but there was little to no theological scholarship specifically about Black millennial women. It made sense—we weren't *scholars* yet in a position to do real research on our generation, and those who were already millennial womanist theologians didn't seem to want to do work specific to our generation. And, to me, their refusal to do work our generation needed felt rooted in the inconvenient truth that we aren't supposed to embody an identity as Black faith-filled—specifically Christian—women different from previous generations. We were supposed to stay in lockstep with everything they did and believed as Black women. For me, honoring that obligation was becoming increasingly difficult.

When I got to Duke, I immediately sought out J. Kameron Carter. I had read his book, *Race: A Theological Account*, while completing my master's thesis on Black Church social programs. I wanted to be able to write as articulately as he did. Once I got to know him better, I'd joke that he wrote and taught in the "third Heaven." I'd go to his office hours with my list of questions, written on paper or listed in my phone. He'd patiently and attentively listen to them and didn't dismiss me as the annoyance I'm pretty sure I was. "Have you read *Sisters in the Wilderness?*" my professor asked me once. I hadn't. He told me I needed to read it to help with the questions I was formulating. I went straight to the divinity school bookstore, purchased it, and read the entire thing over the weekend.

Sisters in the Wilderness was the first book by a womanist theologian I'd intentionally read. I say intentionally because, while Mama let me read her Renita Weems and Iyanla Vanzant books when I was younger and I read womanist works in college, I didn't know they were womanists and I didn't know what womanism meant. Using the story of Hagar to explain the ways Black women experience gendered oppression in this country, *Sisters in the Wilderness* gave me room to ask very pointed questions. What loyalty does God owe Black women? When will Black women experience God's loyalty? Published years before I would understand anything, this book felt like Delores S. Williams wrote it for me. It was more than pivotal to my formation as a thinker. It helped to shape my understanding of myself as a Black woman in this world.

After reading *Sisters in the Wilderness*, I came to Dr. Carter with more questions, which he answered by recommending more seminal womanist texts. When he introduced me to Monica Coleman's book *Making a Way out of No Way* and her essay "Must I Be Womanist?" she became the blueprint for me. Reading her essay, I felt as if she'd heard our complaints from undergrad and worked to make womanism more accessible to the masses of Black women that traditional iterations seemed to leave out. If I was going to be a womanist, I wanted to be one like her.

Through the academy, many of these women I was reading were accessible through conferences, social media, and the church. But reading their works and meeting them sometimes felt disjointed. I was surprised to meet a Black woman who'd written about Black women's resilience and ability to overcome oppressive conditions and have her be cold, distant, and sometimes mean as hell. I hesitate to admit this because I understand Black women have a right to their anger and being "nice" Black women feeds into notions of respectability. Still, these women's standoffishness felt contrary to the Black women's solidarity professed in their work. I'd ultimately learn the silent opinion regarding some within the womanist theological guild was that their work and person weren't in sync. Yet, as I read about the dangers Black women face when attacking sexism and patriarchy within the church and as I experienced my own, I understood better the way sexism and patriarchy had pitted us against one another.

Still, I wanted to be like them. I wanted to write like them. I believed I'd found my voice and my tribe. My goal became to work hard and establish myself as one of the leading womanist theologians in the academy. And as I got more comfortable with the ways womanism would be repudiated by others when fully lived into by Black women, I became even bolder in calling out sexism and clapping back. I'd never had a problem with saying what I felt but, somehow, I'd gotten even bolder. My mouth got even more slick.

Mama hated it. She called me one day and just said, "Come home." She stayed doing that. This time, I couldn't think of anything I'd said on social media, so I prepared myself for the worst. I was afraid she was going to tell me about a bad diagnosis or that something happened to my grandmother. Instead, she confronted me about a Facebook post I wrote calling bible colleges "glorified vacation bible school." I explained to her why I said it; I was tired of these backwoods preachers coming for me. Mama didn't care. She also saw some of the public posts of a few womanist scholars I idolized and thought they were straight-up mean girls and I was becoming like them. "I don't care if their mamas taught them to get every degree in the world and look down on folk with it," she'd say. "That's not who I raised you to be."

Whenever I tried to explain to her what we were up against, she'd shut me down. "You think yall are the only ones who know there's sexism in the church?" she'd ask me. And I had no comeback because I hadn't experienced leaving a church and feeling abandoned because I was single and pregnant. "There's sexism in the world but you don't pour gasoline on the fire to put it out, and you don't have to be ugly to the very people you say you're trying to help."

These two things would stick with me long after the conversation ended, even as I rejected them in the moment. Mama just didn't get it and I couldn't make her get it. But in truth, Mama saw so much more than I realized she did; she saw me becoming an arrogant, elitist bitch. One who flaunted and wielded my education and access, harming the very people I said they served. When it was clear I wasn't listening to her anymore, she'd just shake her head and say she was praying for me. I'd give anything to have those moments back again.

More than anyone, including myself, Mama believed I had

a "big call." When I was no more than five years old, her mentor Pastor McDowell prophesied I was destined to become a social scientist. Mama said she didn't pay enough attention to the social sciences while in college to know what their graduates did. But when I found my footing in sociology, Mama smiled and was happy to see the fulfillment of the prophecy. She understood my enrollment in seminary as an extension of that call, and yet she wanted it to be *my* call. Whenever folks would push me into preaching, Mama would become extremely resistant. Since the majority of her favorite preachers were women, and a few of her close homegirls were preachers themselves, I knew it wasn't because she was against women in the pulpit. Thanks to Mama, I was raised on the preaching of women like Bishops Iona Locke, Carolyn Showell, Jackie McCullough, and Juanita Bynum. Maybe because I didn't carry myself like those women—because I stayed in trouble in school—Mama didn't think I was called. But that wasn't it at all.

My mama felt whatever I was called to do would include the church but she didn't want me to be bound by it. "God is bigger than the four walls of the church and what you're supposed to do is for outside as much as it is for inside of those walls." She'd speak those words over me until she had no more breath to say anything.

I had a mother who believed in my gifts and talents, believed they were called to shake things up, *and* believed I could be kind while doing it. She didn't believe in calling someone out. Mama favored the notion of "bringing someone to" something. By being direct, clear, kind, and compassionate, she believed you could provoke someone's awareness and change their hearts. She had much more faith in people than I ever could and she knew more than I did what womanist theology could do. She'd been reading it for as long as I'd been alive. She knew how it served her and knew its power to serve other women. Reading Iyanla Vanzant and Renita Weems empowered my mother to believe her current circumstances weren't her final destination. She understood the room Black women give each other to call out our foolishness in love so we can become the best versions of ourselves. That's what those books and magazine columns did for her and so many others. And she knew what womanism could do for and *through* me if I got out of my own way. To tell the truth, it was witnessing Mama read books and the *Essence* columns written by Vanzant, Weems, and Susan L. Taylor that inspired me to become a writer. I wanted to do for Black women my age what they'd done for my mother's generation.

But getting out of my way would prove difficult the further I wanted to go in academic womanist theological discourse. I identified those who were considered the gatekeepers and those dubbed the shining stars and future of the guild and I emulated them. In some instances, I was able to create relationships with them offline and outside of the classroom. I wanted their acceptance and endorsement. They had the command, respect, and fear of Black Church practitioners and academics that I craved. Despite the fact I'd already been a public writer for a few years, I didn't have their stamp of approval and believed I needed it. If I could be crowned by them, I would be unstoppable.

Folks sing the praises of mentorship—I mean, when you get a good mentor, it's great—but very few talk about its woes, about the inherent inequality and power dynamics in those relationships. It's unfair for mentors to treat mentees as if they lack the capacity to teach their mentors anything. I found it hard to get folks to discuss what happens when a mentor is wounded by her own experiences and carries that baggage into the mentoring dynamic. It's rare to find honest discourse about the damage wounded Black women mentors can do. It's one of those unspoken rules (like sitting still in the dark when it's "thundering and lightning" outside): speaking publicly about professional and accomplished Black women's wounds is profoundly disrespectful.

There are a lot of wounds in womanist theology, and rightfully so. Wounded by those in the academy, the community, and the church, and by other Black women, womanist theologians have good reason to be pissed. Those wounds don't negate or dismiss their contributions and neither should we; that's what got us here. They are the Hagars God sent back into oppression with only a promise. Some have made the best lives they could from that promise. I wonder, though, how many have counted the cost of mentoring us this way. How do we talk honestly about what it's like to be molded by broken women? Admittedly, I'm still trying to figure it out myself. Even here, I'm doing my best to be gracious, not name anyone, and walk the tightrope of respect and truth.

Being molded by scorned women hurts. It hurt me to seek out affirmation and wisdom from a mentor and be confronted instead by her resentment that I didn't have to endure what she did to get where I was. "All the work we did to build up this discourse, and these publishers are just passing over us to give yall book deals. I've been writing and working for thirty years," she said. "All you do is tweet. I guess it's just a different time." Stunned, I didn't know what to say.

Mentors leading wound-first can be prone to shaping their mentees into who they wish they would have been if given the mentees' timing and opportunities. And this guidance is not necessarily from a loving space. *Preach this way. Don't talk about this online. Lose weight. Don't cut your hair. Don't look too masculine presenting.* They struggle to identify the ways showing up in the world is just different for us now. We're choosing to engage in ministry differently. Some of the difference is a function of being millennials, meaning we're going to do what we want and not be beholden to tradition and status quo. But our transformed approaches are greatly influenced by our having witnessed how their ministering, teaching, and leadership styles damaged them and refusing to let the same happen to us.

I know this struggle isn't exclusive to womanist theology or the academy itself. Sisters in other fields have been victim of this unhealthy dynamic as well. Mama would often repeat the statement "Nurses eat their young." It was her way of talking about the ways young nurses were often hazed and treated bad by their older colleagues. Mama would also talk often about her Black female supervisor who, she said, taught her how to be treacherous. Ma said it was because her supervisor had been passed over for jobs and promotions. By the time Mama's generation of nurses came along, she said, broader cultural mindsets and policies had changed in ways that directly benefited them. New hires could go further faster, and their supervisors resented them for it.

While Mama understood the animosity, she wasn't here for it and she couldn't understand the hazing. She said her supervisor would do things to try to make her quit. When she didn't, her boss finally found a way to balance her respect and disgust. But Mama also saw it when she transitioned to the academy. She often recalled the dissertation defense she attended at the institution where she was completing her doctorate in nursing. With their brutal questions and condescending demeanor, the Black women scholars in her field reduced a grown woman to a puddle of tears. When they finished their questions and began deliberating on her defense, Mama watched one of her classmates collapse into her mother's and children's arms. Grandma told her not to worry because nothing remotely close to it would happen at Mama's defense. "Nobody is going to embarrass *my* child in front of me!" Grandma was adamant. We tried to explain to her, even though we hated it, that hazing was part of the process. Some Black women scholars just believed you had to go through whatever they'd endured to earn your PhD. They had the opportunity to do something different, make it right, but they didn't. And you don't say a word about it. You just cuss them out in your group chats, within the safe space of your girls, who understand your plight and won't tell a soul.

My relationships with many womanist theologians were complicated to say the least. While I desperately sought their approval, I also had a slick mouth. Though I believe in deference, if your name isn't Debra Louise Benbow, you can't talk to me like you're crazy and have me accept it. I was constantly told I didn't know my place. I was "skipping" line and not paying enough dues. The women who said these things felt justified when I left my doctoral program. When the news spread through those circles of women I thought were friends and mentors, they proved to be nothing more than gossips who rattled off what they'd heard and added to it. Some of them were bold enough to reach out to me to tell me that when their mothers died, they still found ways to complete their programs.

Likewise, after I ended up in the hospital for suicidal ideation and major depression, several women told me they'd endured hospitalization, fled abusive marriages with their children in tow, and were still able to complete their programs. All of this was to reinforce the notion that I wasn't working hard enough through my trauma to get the degree. If they did it, I should have been able to do it, too.

That's when it landed for me: I didn't want to be like them after all. I wanted to be whole and I wanted to be well. I couldn't be those things pursuing a doctorate anymore. Things completely shifted for me, and I was okay with walking away, even if it meant being a failure in their eyes.

Womanist theology gave me the language to best articulate Black women's relationship with God, and it gave me permission to honor and explore my own unconventional spirituality, but it did not give me my ethics or sense of purpose. Mama, my grandma, aunties, Sunday School teachers, and the other Black women in my life growing up did that.

There are amazing people within the academic guild of womanist theology. I want to be clear about that. When Monica Coleman became not just a scholar whose words I lived by but a dear friend, I knew I hit the jackpot. When she helped me navigate returning home and reclaiming my life after hospitalization, it was clear that womanist theology wasn't just a point of entrance into a conversation for her but a way of life. And she isn't the only one. Many women I met during my time in the academy were very good to me.

But in the wake of everything I'd lost, I wanted to reclaim the parts of me with some semblance of wholeness before everything was burned in the fire. To do that, I'd need to reconnect with people who knew me before I began chasing whatever success I thought I'd find being an acclaimed womanist scholar. I'd need the people who knew me when my dreams were big and my spirit and heart were unbroken. I'd need my girls.

I'd need my group chats. My oldest friends from childhood, my girls from Tennessee State, my line sisters and sorors, my squads from church and grad school. They knew me before life broke me and they know me well. I leaned on them to find myself and put myself back together. They gave me the room to become undone and be an entire mess. And they could mark ways I was growing and evolving into the best possible version of myself. I needed the sisters I'd met along the way who got me. In the fires of grief and trauma, our relationships were battle-tested and showed me what sisterhood is supposed to look like. Through them, I understood how my mama was able to give me so many aunts.

All them heffas got slick mouths too, though, and it can get a little steamy when I'm in the hot seat—because they had no problems telling me they weren't fans of the elitist academic snob I was becoming. My aunties couldn't stand it either. Before she passed, Ma would have Aunt Jan spy on my Facebook page and comments. After Mama died and Aunt Jan would send a random "checking in" text, I knew it was her way of lovingly asking me to pull back from social media a bit because she knew Mama would want her to and, eventually, I would appreciate it. And I did.

I know it's from a place of love. Audria calling to say, "Bitch, get your shit together" when I'm being a hot mess, is an act of endearment. When Leah and D'Najah start their comments with "friend . . ." or Indhira calls me "beloved," I know I'm doing the most. I usually take a deep breath and prepare myself before I read Micky's and Aja's texts outside our group chats because they're probably getting me together for the ways I've been living underneath my potential and need to do better. Shamel, Shannon, Angela, Melissa, and India will all tell me it's okay while DeAnna will give it to me straight. And Crystal, Chanelle, and Shonquila are always going to be my alibi. All of my girls bring me back to myself.

Relationships with Black women are complicated, mainly because we're human and we will make mistakes. There are some sisters I don't rock with because they hurt me. There are some sisters who don't rock with me because I hurt them. In our woundedness, we have been harmful. What distinguishes us are the ways we own it, apologize, and attempt to grow.

I hate how the statement "Black women will save us" gets

used to explain the numerous times we've come to the aid of this country and to communities and individuals who barely (if ever) care for us in the ways we care for them. Yet, I know intimately how true the statement is. I have been saved time and again by Black women. They've helped me just like Mama helped my auntie that night. When I was ready to leave the pain of New Jersey, my line sister Keisha simply said, "Come here and take all the time you need." I moved to Atlanta with no plan, just the love and support of my sister. In our relationships with one another, Black women have been the bridges over troubled waters we've needed.

I may not have always known I was womanist and I may no longer spend my time in spaces where womanist discourse is dominant. But I am womanist. I believe when Black women thrive, the world thrives. And I'm working daily to create a world where that thriving is possible. I still don't know about this "big call" Mama and Pastor McDowell believed I had, but I do know caring for Black women, in whole and respectful ways, has to be at the center of it. In my quest for the bright lights of academic significance, I lost my way. "It's okay, shug," LaSha said to me. "I can guarantee you'll find your way again and will still be doing the most." Oh, how I love Black women.

SURVIVED BY A
SPECIAL FRIEND

Even as a child, I loved homegoing services. The pageantry and care with which Black people send a loved one home are second to none. More than attending the service itself, I enjoyed reading obituaries. Mama thought it was weird I loved them. But, as the last written word honoring someone's life, the obituary is important. Aside from serving legal purposes, obituaries tell us everything we need to know about the deceased. After writing Mama's, I realized how hard it is to write an obituary, trying my best to beautifully craft the final statements about her life. I procrastinated all week until I couldn't anymore. Dustin needed the obit to complete Mama's tribute booklet. "Reverend," he said. "I know you don't want to do this but we've got to get it done." I've yet to find a task more difficult. As a gift to families now, I offer to write the obituary. In a moment where the worst thing has happened, it's the least I can do to help relieve stress.

One particular section of the obituary lists the person's

loved ones. Back in the day it would start with "They are survived by . . ." Now we say fancier things like "Their memory is cherished by," and list everyone special to them. Attending a few funerals with Mama, I noticed some obituaries read, "Survived by a special friend," and listed only one person. I assumed it was grown-up talk for "best friend" until we attended the funeral of one of my mother's good friends, Mr. Tony, and the special friend listed in his obituary wasn't the person who got up to speak and said she was Mr. Tony's best friend. On the ride home, I asked Mama about it. "It's when you love somebody just like you," she said. "If you're a girl and you love a girl. Or if you're a boy and you love another boy," Mama said, because it was illegal for people to marry people who were the same as them, they were called "special friends."

"When I die, am I going to have a special friend?" I asked, still too young to really understand how gender and sexuality worked.

She told me if I was, I would be the first to know it myself. Then she thought about it some more and laughed. "But the way you got Bobby Brown and Tevin Campbell hanging all over that room of yours, I don't think so."

It would take years before I understood what my mother was trying to explain to me. And I knew it wasn't universal; there were times when "special friends" meant best friends—people who had become family. That's what makes recognizing the partners of queer and same-gender-loving folks as "special friends" even more disrespectful. Because using this term wasn't about honoring the loved one who passed away or even respecting the person they loved who was still here. It was about the family attempting to tell the truth without making everyone else uncomfortable. When we sat at those funerals and read those obituaries where lovers and life partners were listed as "special friends," we were witnessing families revise history simply because they were afraid of what the people in attendance would say.

And, sometimes, it wasn't like folks didn't know. What I'd come to learn was, outside of their biological families, same-gender-loving people had to make their own families and become part of communities where they were safe and could thrive among people who knew the truth about them. It was unfortunate, in so many instances, that biological family members would have the final say over a person's last rites. Someone could have grown up in a deeply homophobic family and the person who truly loved them could be fundamentally erased from their final narrative because the ones legally left to tell the story never truly accepted them for who they were.

Ma said there are going to be a lot of surprised folks once we get to Heaven. She said people spend so much time telling us who they think won't be there they forget they're not the ones in charge of the guest list. Something tells me she knew she was in the minority with that perspective.

I was raised believing that the absolute worst thing that you could be was gay. It broke God's heart and disgusted Him. Back then, we didn't have terms like "queer" or "same-gender-loving" to articulate the spectrum of sexuality. Actually, let me take that back. I'm pretty sure the terminology existed and an understanding of those concepts was available; it was just my little corner of the world didn't use them. You were either gay or straight. There was nothing in between. You could love God and you could even want to be like Jesus, but there was no way you were sincere in your commitment as long as you were gay.

From the pulpit, I often heard "God made Adam and Eve and not Adam and Steve." And then, there were times when pastors would get extremely graphic and ask what would a real man want with another man's penis in his mouth. That would sometimes be met with a gasp, but every instance received an "Amen, Pastor!" or a "Tell the truth and shame the devil!" Because, to those pastors and parishoners, it was the truth. The bible was clear: homosexuality is a sin and an abomination. We were supposed to hate what God hates, and God hates sin. Even as a kid, I knew there was no real care or regard for the feelings of queer folk in my church. And they were there. It was interesting how, as long as they were working in the church, their sexuality wasn't an issue, but the moment our pastor would bring it up in a sermon, eyes would dart in their direction. Consequently, I grew up believing heterosexuality gave me some kind of moral superiority. It was the big Joker on my forehead, winning any argument. It didn't matter what I'd done; at least I wasn't gay.

It was understood, even if you loved someone who was gay, they were still sinning and acting in open rebellion against God. I got that but, to me, being gay was no more sinful than lying or stealing. At least the message of no difference was projected by my family and the community organizations

Mama and I belonged to. In God's eyes, there was no difference between a gay person, a drug addict, or an abuser. They were in need of God's love and the support of community to repent and be who God intended.

Although this was a much kinder response than the fire and brimstone I heard in church, it was still wrong. And as much as I didn't want to admit it, this response to same-gender-loving people also meant they actually had been mistreated in and by my family. The benevolent homophobia I learned from my family and from those who considered themselves progressive was just as harmful as anything else.

I can't remember the first time I heard the instruction "Hate the sin . . . Love the sinner," but it was understood as a responsible and ethical Christian approach to homosexuality. It explained that while God hates sin, God loves the one committing the sin. God's love for gay people creates the capacity with which they can overcome their sin and be made whole. Consequently, they'll escape Hell.

The overwhelming and transformative love of God would bring them out of sin, just as it had brought us out. And, whenever we saw someone denounce their sexuality and same-gender attraction, we were supposed to rejoice because the renunciation meant that they had allowed their devotion to God to match God's devotion to them. This was the wrong approach. Full stop. It made sense and seemed kind to me only because it didn't affect my lived reality. I didn't wrestle with my sexuality or an attraction to other women in a way that made me question my identity and self-worth or forced me to live in secrecy and shame. Looking back, I see that my pious arrogance was hilarious given my own life was a hot mess at the time.

Like when I got out of a dude's bed to go into his living room to pray my friend out of lesbianism. In college, she asked me if I ever thought about being with a woman. Sure, I'd *thought* about it. We watched *BET: Uncut* before bed and hip-hop videos had become their own not-so-soft-core pornos sensationalizing two girls kissing. And even though we'd joked about what kind of girls we liked (I was partial to thick chicks who were built like the best of what the South had to offer), I thought we were just joking. I was having a hard enough time repenting for these dudes on my roster; I couldn't add a girl into the mix and jeopardize my walk entirely.

But it was becoming more clear to me that for her none of these things were funny. She liked women, she wanted to be with them, and she knew it was wrong. She asked me to be part of her accountability team. Whenever she had the urge to be with a woman or those feelings would take over, she could call us and we would drop everything and pray with her. We knew her SOS calls were matters of life and death. When I came back in the dude's room after calling on the strong name of Jesus and rebuking the spirit of lust and homosexuality, he looked at me like I was crazy, shook his head, and laughed while asking for some head. It would be years before I realized how ridiculous the entire night was. My friend, who eventually married the very person I was praying God would deliver her from, laughs about it to this day.

As I grew and journeyed through my early twenties, I thought that loving LGBTQIA+ people the best way I could was my role in helping them find their way back to God. That meant leaning further into the false moral high ground the church tried to offer, that I was better than gay people simply because I was straight. In so many ways, church pit single Black women and queer people, more specifically gay Black men, against each other. The "down low" phenomenon and "all these gay men turning brothers out" were said to be the reasons women in my mother's generation couldn't find good men. And when Black women had begun to contract HIV at alarming rates, the narrative formed that they couldn't trust these men to be straight, and, if sisters just devoted themselves to God and the church, a saved, heterosexual Black man would come their way. The longer the years dragged on without these hetero Black Prince Charmings, the more women grew resentful and made gay Black men in the church their proverbial punching bags.

But there's another lingering frustration that single, cisgender, heterosexual Black women have toward Black LGBTQIA+ people that has little to do with our shrunken dating pools. Black queer people, by virtue of naming themselves as such, get to live into a sexual freedom and liberation that single Black Christian women are told cannot be ours. We heard if we delight ourselves in the Lord, our hearts' desires would be made manifest. Well, what happens when we keep working and serving, being faithful to God, and go home to empty houses and no one to love us? And what are we supposed to make of this difference when the ones who are "abominations" have partners to hold and love them?

I'm not delusional or trying to insinuate all Black queer

people are able to express their sexuality freely and without harm. We know they're not. As homophobia and queer and trans antagonism steadily rise, Black LGBTQIA+ folks remain terrifyingly vulnerable to all forms of violence, and the one place where they should be safe, the church, they are not. And as Black queer folks are still under assault and attack, I know single Black Christian women who struggle underneath pastors' instructions to deny themselves pleasure and intimacy. I know women who still believe a woman cannot be touched until a man has named her his wife, and refuse to pile years of guilt and shame onto themselves should they give in to temptation before matrimony. And rather than call out the pastors who traffic in this nonsense, they find it easier to point fingers at gay Black men for their epidemic of singleness. Internalizing this hatred weds them even tighter to their superiority complex: We may be single. We may be lonely. We may even be forsaking our own needs out of some misplaced allegiance to the church and its leaders. But at least we won't lift up our single, lonely, disillusioned eyes in Hell.

I didn't realize how much I believed this. Even as I was thotting and bopping in and out of beds in the hope of a happily ever after, I believed I was doing this in full alignment with God's intention for me. The fact that it wasn't panning out for me the way it was for unrepentant sinners was mind-boggling. Not only had I drunk the church's Kool-Aid but I'd begun to make more whenever my pitcher was running low.

Community changed my life. Actually, it saved my life, because through the wonder of community, I was able to confront my own homophobia and hypocrisy. Throughout my life, I've had friends who were gay and queer. I've had the honor of friends coming out to me and trusting me with their truth. I wish I could say I handled all those revelations correctly, but I didn't. More times than not, I agreed to be part of friends' accountability groups to "pray the gay away." I cosigned when they told me they were going to keep their sexuality hidden. Many times, I encouraged this decision. At first, it was "We're in high school and coming out can make it hard." Then, it was "Do you really know these folks won't spread your business across campus?" After that, it was "We're trying to get jobs and start our careers . . . now may not be the time." I pushed my friends further into closets and despair.

Grad school changed everything for me. It was where I met one of my best friends, Derrell Pettiway. I liked him because his mouth was slick just like mine, and we became fast friends. Derrell had a close-knit group of Black gay friends who were all out. Derrell was actually the first "out" gay person I knew who was also my age. I don't know how I came to the conclusion gay people who are out are older but somehow I did. Derrell disrupted all my assumptions. And Derrell was gay and Christian. There was no confusion for him. After reading my life and snatching my edges about whatever guy I was dealing with at the time, he'd say, "Give it to God, girl," and tell me he'd pray for me. If he was confused or wavered about his identity at that time in his life, you wouldn't have known. How Derrell lived his truth made me question everything I knew to be true. It wasn't difficult for him to reconcile being gay and Christian. The tormented battle I was told raged within queer people couldn't be found in Derrell, at least from what I could tell.

There were times when my questions to Derrell bordered on absolutely disrespectful. I couldn't conceive of how he could consider himself Christian and a proud gay Black man. I didn't understand his close friendships with gay Black men who didn't subscribe to flamboyant, over-the-top stereotypes. And whenever my inquiries dipped a little too far toward judgment and scrutiny, Derrell had no problem getting me to-gether. I wasn't better than him because I was straight. He let me know I was bumbling and fumbling in love just like every-body else.

One time, I'd defensively told Derrell he had to give people time to grow and unlearn because embracing "the homosex-ual lifestyle" might be new to them. Derrell paused, sat back in his chair, and straightened out his clothes like he knew he was about to read me for filth. Quietly, he asked me how long it took me to learn the new guy's telephone number and favor-ite foods. He asked me how much time I needed to clean my apartment when dude called out the blue and said he's com-ing over. "How much time did it take you to forget you said the last one was 'the one' before you started saying *this* dude is?" (Okay, that one *still* kinda stings.)

Then Derrell looked me in my face and asked, "How much time do I get as your friend?" If I could give these other men time and intention in dead-end relationships, why couldn't I put the same effort into respecting my friend—one of the few men who has never let me down? It was then I realized, no matter how much I thought I wasn't the problem, my belief that LGBTQIA+ folk should be patient while straight folk evolve means I was indeed the problem.

For Derrell, for other people I love, and for myself, I wanted to be better. We call it being "allies" now. And, while I believe allyship is important and while I also believe only the people you're advocating for can call you an ally, I mostly just want to be a better human. My commitment requires I advocate alongside people in marginalized communities, allowing them to hold me accountable so I can be a part of creating the world I believe God has always wanted us to actualize. My desire to be better also pushed me to look at scripture differently. I stopped fighting folks a long time ago about how they interpret the bible. I choose to lean on the work of queer theologians and biblical scholars Bishop Yvette Flunder, Pamela Lightsey, Darnell Moore, Horace Griffin, and Eric Thomas, whose writings highlight the way religious structures demonize same-gender relationships for the purposes of power and nation-building. It should be common sense for folks, especially when we understand the biblical idea of marriage as solely for the purpose of transferring land and wealth. But there are still biblical literalists who look at scripture as authoritative on the subject. I don't.

But more than my disbelief in biblical inerrancy, I believe in the flawlessness of God's heart. I believe to suggest samegender attraction and queer and trans identity are sinful is to fundamentally betray the heart of a God who created us with intention. A God who created us to live in community. A God who wants us to know who we love is not the totality of who we are. There are some heterosexual folks who are absolute monsters; I believe their actions disappoint God far more than two consenting men being in a loving relationship ever will. Plus, I refuse to believe that God actually cares about what grown people do in their bedrooms as much as people want me to believe God does.

There are people who genuinely ask me how I did it. They want to know how I was able to make this theological shift. The truth is it wasn't easy. Friends like Derrell can push you all day but, in the end, you have to fully turn the corner. I met Derrell while we were both pursuing master's degrees in sociology. I was sitting with data and theories about what marginalization really looks like in the lives of people who are oppressed by structural forces. I couldn't contend with how racism, sexism, and classism limit the possibilities for social mobility and ignore the theological implications of that same stunted mobility. If gender and sexuality are social constructs, then I can't dismiss the fact that the theological justifications used to ground these constructs are also faulty.

I believe God's intention is a flourishing creation. I don't believe God looks at LGBTQIA+ folk and says, "nah . . . not them," simply because their truth contradicts who *we* have decided God is. And, after Derrell read the hell out of me and I gave up my need for a God who fits my criteria, I was introduced to a God more just, empathetic, and kind than I could have imagined. A God who is no less God because people love and live outside of the hierarchies we have created in God's name. A God, I believe, who has allowed for the existence of opportunities and resources for those who need to make necessary changes to the genders assigned to them at birth. I believe what God wants from us is to create a world where all are free to thrive. Anything less doesn't represent God's heart and what God wants for us.

These beliefs are why homophobia, queerphobia, and trans antagonism are among my deal breakers in a relationship. I can't be with a man who believes there is a "gay agenda" or that homosexuality is the emasculation of Black men. Derrell and the people I love in my life deserve better. And so does the world I hope to see.

I cringe when I think of the years I hurt gay and queer people with my harmful theology and willful ignorance. While my life is now filled with a diversity of voices and experiences, some people walked away from me because I wasn't a safe space. That was their right, because I was wrong.

I want a world where the ones coming behind us don't have to fear living into their truth. I want a world where my children can come to me and their father, tell us what they know about themselves, and be met with love and acceptance from both of us. I want a world where my children and their friends and partners won't have to be listed as "special" when they have to say goodbye to love.

BLACK LACE TEDDIES
AND OTHER PIECES I ROCK
UNDER THE ANOINTING

Christians are absolutely obsessed with sex. We've made whether we have it or not our entire worlds. We act like life is over as soon as we find out someone else, mainly someone of the cisgender female persuasion, is having it. Just look at how so many of our families have worked overtime to give the appearance of being the "right" kind of family. Unplanned pregnancies and single mothers put monkey wrenches in our little plans to show the world our families are godly. Parents are still ostracizing young women for being pregnant and unmarried and justifying it as a godly response. Entire theologies and doctrines have been created from sketchy biblical interpretations attempting to prove the Divine Creator wants us to wait until we're married to have sex. We are absolutely obsessed with sex. And I used to live into the obsession.

I'd been a virgin through high school, and you couldn't tell me I wasn't in line to go to college, find a boyfriend, start my career, marry said boyfriend, have a few kids, and live happily ever after—my prize for spending the first eighteen years of my life sex-free. When I got to Tennessee State, I even joined the Chastity League to reinforce my commitment. As soon as I got on campus, I heard the rumors about the girls in the Chastity League—that they were undercover hoes—but those were just the rantings of haters. They couldn't stand the possibility of young college women completely devoting their lives to God and not choosing to be freaks. I was so righteous and pious . . . until spring break of my freshman year, when I "lost" my virginity.

We say "lost my virginity" like we don't know where it went. I know exactly where it is, and I had absolutely no problem saying goodbye to it. I'd fallen in love with a roughneck with a good heart. We were such the church girl/bad boy cliché, but we were young and in love. And taking our relationship to the next level only felt right. But being sexually active made my time in the Chastity League quite complicated. Here I was, getting it in, while my fellow Chastity League sisters were keeping their word to God. I couldn't tell the truth because they would ask me to leave the group, solidifying my eternity in Hell. Instead, I decided to keep my secret and remain a member. When another Chastity League member and I mumbled greetings to each other in passing outside the same football player's campus apartment one night, I knew the campus rumors were true.

I have a confession to make: I only felt bad about having sex because I understood guilt as what I was *supposed* to feel. Contrary to high school girl horror stories, my first time wasn't horrifying. It was beautiful, actually. And I enjoyed it each time we did it. I forced myself to be ashamed because, according to Christian logic, I was committing sin. And this wasn't just regular sin; I was apparently doing irreparable damage to my body and spirit. I was forming a "soul tie."

According to some Christians, a soul tie happens when two people have sex; their souls become connected. According to "soul tie doctrine," this is why sex is solely for marriage; each time you have sex, you and your partner exchange parts of your souls. When you think about it, this is some real top-tier, peak science fiction. I first heard of soul ties in high school, when the women from our church came back from Bishop T. D. Jakes's Woman Thou Art Loosed conference in Atlanta. There, Juanita Bynum preached the sermon "No More Sheets," in which she introduced this concept to those unfamiliar with it. "No More Sheets" took off—shifting how women's ministries (and Black women specifically) understand the pain connected to their sexual experiences. Ultimately, the majority of them went back home from that conference concluding this pain was solely their fault.

I learned more about soul ties in college. The church I joined had an entire ministry focused on this belief. I tried to remain committed to its teaching and became celibate. I really tried. I even participated in the True Love Waits for College Students initiative and got one of those celibacy promise rings. For college graduation, I upgraded it to one with the words "Patiently Waiting" engraved on it. I dreamt of having it made into a watch as a wedding gift for my husband. I lost count of how many times I took it off when I had company and, within the first year, it was completely rusted. I have absolutely no idea where that thing is now.

This ring was quite a prophetic and fitting analogy for my overall commitment to abstinence. I consistently "slipped up." I'm lying. These were *not* slipups. I didn't accidentally find myself in someone else's bed. But, like clockwork, I cried like a baby after we were done. One guy told me I made him feel like "the devil," but when I called and asked him to come back over the following week, he knew everything was all good.

I sat in the uncomfortable tension of believing in my heart that premarital sex wasn't sinful but knowing in my head I was betraying God. What was wrong with me? I wasn't yet ready to accept that it was possible to be my authentic self (which at this point definitely included my libido) *and* be fully loved by God. So I believed I was in open rebellion against God and I didn't know how to get back into God's good graces. I had no true road map. What worked for others—reading the bible and repenting—didn't work for me. I was just broken, I guessed.

My acceptance of soul ties came to an end during my senior year in college. To conclude women's month at church, the co-pastor/first lady instructed us to wear all white and bring items to lay on the altar as sacrificial offerings. I brought letters and pictures from my boyfriend and anything reminding me of my sex life. After we laid down our sacrificial offerings, the co-pastor/first lady gave further instructions. "Let the virgins come." One by one, I watched as girls who were waiting until they were married danced at the altar and did something I could not do for myself: with their pure bodies in motion, they made my offering acceptable to God. I left the service convinced there was a level of connection with God I'd never get back, simply because I wasn't a virgin anymore.

On the way home, I called Mama to talk through it. "Was there a golden calf, too?" Mama asked. We both laughed, but I was serious. So was Mama. She thought the whole ritual was ridiculous and she made it known. "If you sit up there and let them tell you some girls who probably are lying themselves gotta dance on your behalf, you want to feel crazy." I saw her words as permission to let the idea go.

After my conversation with Mama, I began to ask specific questions about soul ties. I couldn't just take the concept at face value anymore. Why was I believing it in the first place? God created us with minds. Aren't we supposed to use them? So many of us have shouted off sermons and lived our entire existences off a preacher's tangents when none of it made sense. Once, my grandmother proved this. I was worshipping with her at our family church, St. Stephen Missionary Baptist Church, and one of her friends said "Amen" and "Preach, Pastor" after every other word. At the end of the sermon, she asked him what the pastor said. He couldn't even tell her and tried to laugh to deflect attention from his embarrassment. Grandma said, "Folks will say the sky is purple knowing that it's blue just because the pastor said it." As others nodded in agreement, she told her friend, "God gave you your own brain. Sometimes, you need to use it."

In that same spirit, I would finally interrogate the soul tie doctrine "unsuccessfully" running my life.

How are soul ties broken? It seemed like every pastor gave me a different answer to this question. Some pastors said that being able to break a soul tie depended on the person you'd had sex with and the type of intercourse. Others gave this laundry list of both confusing and exhausting steps that included extreme fasting, personal isolation, and simply becoming weird as hell in the name of redemption. A few went as far as to say breaking a soul tie is impossible. This idea that there are bonds even the blood of Jesus couldn't break made no sense to me. And yet, it was preached as the consequence of doing something you know you're not supposed to do. Ultimately, pastors doubled down on this fact: if you weren't having sex with people who weren't your spouse, you wouldn't have to worry about getting a soul tie in the first place.

What about victims of rape and incest? Again, I received different answers. Some pastors were adamant God doesn't allow victims of rape to form soul ties with their rapists. Others were also clear: rape is sexual intercourse and, through intercourse, soul ties are formed. So, in one instance, God would block the soul tie from forming but wouldn't stop the violence from taking place. And, in the other instance, God simply didn't care. Obviously, there were genuine inconsistencies in a doctrine I was using to guide my life, a doctrine which didn't reflect the God I believed in.

Even after the women came back from Woman Thou Art Loosed those years ago, my mother rarely missed an opportunity to tell me how nonsensical she thought the notion was. And she didn't need to track it through scripture; she could lean on her own experience. Mama was clear: she didn't have a soul tie with my father. She had one with *me*. Mama believed soul ties were between parents and children. Granted, she didn't tell me this when I was younger. My conversations about sex with Ma when I was an adult were much different from the ones I had with her in my childhood years and during college. She understood she was raising a Black girl in the 1990s. She had to protect me from the influences and dangers of the outside world. Predators left very few spaces for Black girls to be safe. Maybe telling me you could get pregnant from kissing was only part of the story; even still, I got why she did it. (And I plan to be a little more communicative than my mama was when it's time to discuss this with my own children.)

When it came to physical intimacy, my mother never really answered my questions, and I had a lot of them. I was in elementary school when a friend detailed the events she'd watched on a porn tape from her father's collection, and I was naïve and ridiculous enough to ask Mama about it. As her reply, she made me watch a video on reproductive health and left the room while it was on. I can sing the theme song to this day. When Mama came back into the room, she asked if I had any questions. The video included footage of a live birth, and I was *traumatized*. Hell no, I didn't have any questions!

Though it was hilarious to reminisce on how this registered nurse fumbled through a sex discussion with her daughter, I wasn't a child anymore and I needed to stop approaching sex as such. Debunking the myth of soul ties and having more honest conversations with Mama led me to real moments of self-discovery. The more I was reading and educating myself, the clearer it became that a robust sex education required wide and directed study. Contrary to what was taught in Sunday School, I shouldn't be learning about sex and sexuality from Leviticus and 1 Corinthians. I needed to study human sexuality and psychology. And I needed a therapist who could help me unpack the foolishness about sex I believed thanks to the church.

And, as great as coming to those realizations was, there was still a problem. I was a budding Black feminist, working to decolonize my mind, but I had not yet allowed my body to be free. I didn't know what brought me joy or pleasure. Sure, I enjoyed sex and I knew what felt good when guys did it. But I didn't know what really made me *happy*. So, what did I do? I turned to books, porn, and toys to more intimately get to know my body. My body belonged to no one else but me, and I wasn't satisfied with just owning it. I needed to fully understand exactly what was in my possession. As I explored, I found what positions and experiences I liked best, and I made sure I received them when I was intimate with someone. Knowing myself in this way was absolute life. And I could articulate this all day from a Black feminist perspective— because sisters have a right to know joy and pleasure in a world which seeks to take those feelings from us. But finding a theological perspective on this aspect of life would take me some more years of reading and thinking.

Reclaiming sexuality and sensuality is seen as solely a feminist move; people believe it has nothing to do with scripture. I believed that, too, until I read women like Monique Moultrie and Jennifer Wright Knust. While I was in seminary, my homeboy Jamal told me to read Moultrie's dissertation, "Between the Horny and Holy: Womanist Sexual Ethics and the Cultural Productions of No More Sheets." When I got to the section where she said, "If Bynum or those influenced by her fame could instead envision a sexual message that encouraged all forms of sexual pleasure and expression, I doubt Black women would struggle as much with the sexual decisions they face," I shouted.* I'd been waiting so long for this.

Lines like "A new womanist relational sexual model will begin with an affirmation of black women's bodies as sexual and spiritual . . . this is done with the knowledge that sexual agency is serious work" inspired me to believe I could write similar papers, though at the time I had no idea what my "work" was. I just had a lot of questions.

Ironically, it was my married situationship who suggested I seek answers in Jennifer Wright Knust's book *Unprotected Texts: The Bible's Surprising Contradictions About Sex and Desire*— thereby introducing me to one of the greatest blessings of my life. Through Knust's exploration of scripture's complex histories and context concerning sex and sexuality, I gained the confidence to say, the bible isn't as "clear" as many like to claim. More important, Knust was an ordained Baptist preacher. Coming from my same denomination, she knew what women like me were up against and helped to give me scriptural support to back up my claims.

These groundbreaking texts finally relieved mounting tensions between my head and my heart. Feeling shame for being

---

* M. N. Moultrie, "Between the Horny and Holy: Womanist Sexual Ethics and the Cultural Productions of No More Sheets" (doctoral dissertation, Vanderbilt University, 2010), 150.

sexual didn't make sense because it wasn't supposed to. Rather, I was learning to see my sexuality as whole and good. Finally, my body began to feel free—free from the shackles of religious oppression and cultural expectations, free to bloom in whatever direction it wanted. More than my response to a wack classmate, these texts truly gave birth to red lip theology as a guiding principle for my life.

Black feminist literature and theory broadened my horizons and my vocabulary for finding synergy. But while womanist theology gave me the language of my faith and religious expression, I still felt constrained by its purported ideals of Black womanhood. It felt like womanism preferred a certain "kind" of Black woman—a respectable one. And that didn't quite reflect me or sisters thinking like me. Though the womanists loved to publicly claim her, Monique Moultrie's sexual ethic—honoring various forms of intimate decision-making—was more for those sisters the womanists would overlook. Creating a freeing sexual ethic for myself and offering it to my homegirls was essential for me.

These cornerstone teachings cemented the truths of my red lip theology in place: (1) Intimacy is holy. (2) God created us for interdependence and connection. When we honor that, we thrive. (3) Intimacy is necessary. (4) Touch is vital. (5) Sex is healthy, necessary, and productive for reasons beyond reproduction. (6) God respects our agency. (7) Those of us who have the privilege of experiencing physical intimacy should do so as often as we deem necessary for our health, wellness, and desires. (8) People who identify as asexual and those for whom intimacy can be difficult because of physical and emotional limitations are no less valuable or important than those who experience intimacy privilege.

One of the first things women ask me when I name these as my truths is how I got here. First, I'm honest. In my teens and twenties, I'd tried to make myself believe what the church said about sex. But it never "took" because reducing God's delight or disappointment in me to whether or not I had sex just seemed very, very dumb. To be a "good" Christian, I was going against my truest self. And the super Saints love to say this is the hallmark of Christianity; we're supposed to walk away from our "sinful" nature, and, according to them, I wasn't doing that. But when I stood in the authenticity of God's creation of me, I couldn't honestly say sex before marriage was wrong.

Beyond that, I'd matured past absorbing juvenile theological positions without proper vetting. (I mean . . . Song of Solomon is right there, within the sixty-six books, talking about sex, and we act like it isn't!) Black people, Black women especially, have a myriad of ways besides scripture to articulate our salvation. Culture and experience—both communal and individual—have always mattered. And I incorporate all of those elements in designing the fullest picture of my faith.

I believe our sexual agency should honor who God created us to be. This is why I don't believe premarital sex is inherently sinful. To me, any intentional act meant to disrupt our flourishing and block the light from within us is what is sinful. I believe that having sex before I'm married, with someone I deeply care about, is not sinful. Often, when women take this posture, it's assumed that they'll sleep with any and every one.

Now be clear: I don't think hookups or opportunities to experience physical intimacy are necessarily sinful, either. I do believe interactions which allow us, Black women especially, to be touched and pleasured are holy. We deserve those kinds of experiences. But just because you think I look good and I think you're fine doesn't mean we're going to sleep together.

To me, having sex to remain in a relationship with someone I know doesn't care about me or any sexual encounter that doesn't serve my highest good and allow me to be my best self *is* sin. And I say this as someone who doesn't shame one-night stands or seasons I like to call "hoebaticals." I ask myself whether I can deal with the implications of temporary hookups, and my answers usually depend on where I am in my life at the time. If I have the emotional bandwidth, it's a go. If I know I don't have the bandwidth and I choose to hook up anyway, I'm being a hot mess. Unless my desires place people (including myself) in physical harm and danger or require manipulation, I don't believe God cares much about my sex life. Sexual violence, pedophilia, and rape culture anger God. Ultimately, I think God cares whether I'm a fundamentally good human being. I think it's more important to God whether I'm treating my neighbor and the stranger as God instructs us. And I sincerely believe that God cares more about whether I'm engaging in relationships with integrity—not lying, cheating, or intentionally hurting my partner through physical or emotional abuse—than God cares about how much me and my boo are getting it in. It's through *those* actions—not whether I waited until my wedding night—that my character and heart are made known.

This is where folks have tuned me out, said I'm not Christian, and demanded I justify my perspective with scripture. They completely ignore my faith approach. But with the perspective of our community's marginalized at the forefront, I don't read the bible the same way they do. I am as Christian as I am feminist as I am Black. There is no parsing out of these identities; they inform one another. So when people dismiss this as an impossibility, I have no problem dismissing them. You can't be in community with me and refuse to respect how I live into my faith, especially when living into it is about the freedom and liberation of people who have suffered under religion's thumb. It doesn't work that way.

Freedom from harmful doctrines is inherently messy. It's transgressive and disrupts every social norm we know. It wouldn't be freedom if it was universally accepted. But here's what I know: a lot of women agree with me (secretly if they must), but they can't let go of the two to whom they've pledged their loyalty and trust, David and Paul: the two men Christians love more than Jesus Christ. Have you ever noticed how much more we quote their words over Jesus's? And that's not just because Paul wrote the majority of the New Testament. We take Paul's words as if Jesus said them. Instead of saying, "Jesus is silent here and we should let his life speak," we fill the silence with everything else.

I get that people love David and Paul—they were both trifling as hell and God still used them. But as beautiful as Psalm 51 seems and as powerful as Galatians 5 may be to some, why would we allow words men wrote in their most vulnerable state to become the standard by which we shape our lives? Nathan confronted David about the liberties he'd taken with Bathsheba, her subsequent pregnancy, and the murder of her husband to cover it up. Realizing his foolishness had been aired out, David cries he was "born into sin and shaped in iniquity." I get why *he* said it; he'd done some really treacherous stuff. But why does David having been a murderous thot make me sinful at birth?

And then there's Paul. We know his story. He persecuted the burgeoning church, God changed his life, and he became one of the greatest saints to ever live. That's great for him, but he literally *killed* Christians. His victims are still dead, and nothing can change that. I've always believed Paul's overzealousness was his attempt to reckon with the harm of his painful past. I can understand that. Still, his testimony ain't mine. Why do I have to form my faith on the basis of the words of trifling men?

David and Paul were jerks. They were men who didn't truly value women and lived quite well into the "humble brag" so many of us hate. They truly believed their own hype, and we've immortalized them—even the women they deride in their missives treasure their words as sacrosanct. Rahab, Ruth, and Vashti—now *these* are the biblical figures who should ground how women understand our sexual agency. But we pledge allegiance to David and Paul, not just because they're men but because we don't love ourselves. And because so many of our faith teachings are grounded in the Calvinistic idea of "total depravity," essentially that we are nothing but "filthy rags" and unrepentant sinners who need God's love to make us whole. This is bad enough, but it reinforces harmful conceits about Black people's sexuality that White folk stressed during enslavement—namely the belief that Black women are no more than wanton seductresses and Black men are nothing but big bucks controlled by what's between their legs. Black people could never be pure or holy. Those virtues were reserved for White people, and those White people exhausted every effort to ensure we didn't experience true intimacy. The reclamation of our right to healthy sexuality and true intimacy is the work our ancestors could not complete. It is our Sankofa.

God created us with loving intention. We are not our "sins" or our shortcomings. We are whole people. Calvinism and other theologies which enforce nonexistent insufficiencies are exactly what keep single Black women on altars praying for husbands and lying in beds alone because they believe doing so makes them righteous in God's eyes. We are not filthy rags. We are living, breathing human beings who God created to experience life—every facet of life—together.

I have friends and know women who have not had sex yet—and that decision is extremely admirable. Some are waiting to have sex because it's the commitment they made to God and themselves. Some are waiting because they still believe it's what you're supposed to do. Even when what they're doing sounds suspect, I don't poke fun at or judge the motives of others. I just want them to make these decisions from a whole and informed place. Many people are wrestling with desires and fighting against fulfilling them. I respect everyone's positions and boundaries. Still, I maintain physical intimacy is a necessary component of a healthy relationship prior to marriage—for me if not for anyone else. I will not limit my understanding of how the Divine can communicate with me. With us.

I wish we lived in a world where Christian identity wasn't focused on our sexual activity. It would have made life much easier for my mother when she was pregnant. It would have made life much easier for me when I was trying to force myself to be contrite and repentant. It would make life much easier for so many. Because sex is only *one* part of our lives. It is a beautiful and fulfilling part, for sure. But there will always be more to us than sex. Anyone who says otherwise isn't deserving of indulging in it.

LEAVING CHURCH

Mama's death rocked me to my core. My mother died alone and, no matter how much I hear the "all things work together" verse in my lifetime, I will always believe she deserved better than that kind of death. Trying to make sense of my mother's fate was actually impossible. I kept recalling the sermons I'd heard about God giving you the desires of your heart if you delight yourself in God. The way Christianity was presented to me led to the understanding that doing good means you get God's choicest blessings. Granted, the older I got, the more I came to know better. I knew life wasn't black-and-white. Being a Christian doesn't exempt you from life's traumas and tragedies. But this was my mother, and none of that mattered.

Despite consistent church attendance and a relatively robust spiritual life, I had nothing to help me navigate the depths of pain caused by Mama's death. It was unimaginable and all-encompassing. Religious platitudes didn't help. I remembered the things people say when folks die; they said them to me when Mama died. *God will never put more on you than you can bear. God took her because He knew she was ready. Satan knows his time is running short so he's trying everything.* (I still don't understand what that means.) I recited the "helpful" scriptures until I was blue in the face. *The Lord gives and the Lord takes away; blessed be the name of the Lord* (Job 1:21). *For everything, there is a season and a time for every matter under Heaven* (Ecclesiastes 3:1). *Blessed are the dead who die in the Lord . . . for they rest from their labor and their works follow them* (Revelation 14:13). I knew these verses by heart and deeply understood how powerful they could be in the right circumstances. Still, in the face of living my worst nightmare, none of them offered solace.

I didn't understand why my mother was gone. Why did *she* die? I found myself drafting a list of relatives God could have taken instead of her. I didn't understand why God took that particular parent when my nonexistent and absent one was available and I would not have missed him as much. In hindsight, people can tell you this practice really isn't productive and that's probably true. Still, I'd become fixated on considering the uses of God's time that would have been better than taking my mama. So much shifted as a result of her death, and none of those shifts were for the better. Everything, for me anyway, just got worse.

To put it bluntly: I lost my mind. I know the shouting cue in church is "I *almost* lost my mind *but* God kept me." Even now, I can hear the chord the organist knows will extend church by at least twenty minutes when played, thanks to a good praise break. And while many can thank God they were able to keep their minds through all the hell they endured, my truth is, for a time, I actually lost mine. *And* I'm still here.

There was no way, I concluded, I could remain whole and live in freedom if I lied about any part of my loss. And many parts of the journey were ugly. Yet, God remained faithful and ever present.

I didn't care how messy or chaotic my grief felt or appeared to others. They didn't have to live my life. What I despised, however, was the commentary from people whose mothers were alive and well or from those who hadn't processed their own loss. Mama hadn't even been gone eighteen months when a friend, an ordained campus chaplain, told me my life lacked discipline. As I described to another friend the weight of emotions I was experiencing, she told me my feelings weren't facts. Yet another friend flat-out told me I needed to learn how to "grieve well." Their mothers were alive and, even if some of them didn't have the greatest relationships, they had no room to criticize how I suffered without mine. As one continued to tell me how she felt about my grief journey, I blurted, "Bitch, your mama is still alive. Holla at me when she's not." We haven't talked since.

And then there were those whose mothers *had* died. They told me it would get easier soon. I understood what they meant but I didn't agree. I'd lost my mama, not a job. I would be experiencing the ebb and flow of sorrow for the rest of my life. There was also the "mentor" who took me to lunch to tell me I needed to grieve in a way that reflected how well my mother raised me. "You want her to look down and be proud of you," she said. Immediately, I was flushed with shame and fear at the thought that my mother was possibly disappointed in how I was grieving her when all I was doing was my absolute best to make it through each day without her. But, as the moment wore off, I realized this instruction was probably one of the dumbest things I'd ever heard. It was stupid and I said as much. We haven't talked since, either.

To many, I was a lost cause. Fodder for their gossip mills. They loved to tell me they were "praying" for me. I'd often ask what they were praying for. I didn't care anymore, and my mouth was reckless. It actually betrayed the last thing my mother said to me. On the evening before she passed away, she called to tell me there had been a terrorist attack in Paris and one of my childhood church friends, who was also one of Mama's faculty colleagues, was in Paris. Immediately, I feared the worst, but Mama assured me Jasmine was okay. She knew Jasmine was okay because she'd called Jasmine herself. In the middle of a terrorist attack, my mama picked up the phone and called her. She was relieved when she heard Jasmine's voice and then chastised her for answering the phone. After hanging up with her, Mama called Jasmine's mother, Mrs. Dianne, to let her know she was there for whatever she needed.

As Mama recounted her conversations with Jasmine and Mrs. Dianne, I scrolled Facebook and became enraged. There were so many people, including our former pastor, saying God did this to get our attention and this is what happens when the world turns its back on God's way. "That is so dumb," I grunted. And then I went into a full-on rant about how people put ridiculous things on God and have no idea the damage their statements make. Mama listened and then simply said, "Candice, you need to be nicer to people." I'd heard a variation of this before, so I settled into what would be a lecture I almost knew by heart. But this one was different.

Mama told me people are doing the best they can to make sense of tragedies and loss. They're trying to help others make sense of these things, too. "They may not have the best tools," she said. "But they're using what they have to try to help somebody." I rolled my eyes—proof people weren't being equipped with better tools, I thought. "Just be nicer because, one day, people are going to be saying the same things to you." I didn't know "one day" would be the next day. I don't think Mama did, either. But Spirit knew. God definitely knew.

So when I would ask, "What exactly are you praying for?" I knew I wasn't exhibiting the kindness Mama had asked I show in what were her final hours. Mama had a faith in people I didn't and, even though she knew firsthand that church people could be trifling, she chose to see the best in folks. I wasn't there, yet. I was young but had a long memory and knew "I'm praying for you" was peak Black Church shade. Those who didn't stutter and lie their way through an answer were honest and told me they were praying for me to get it together. What was clear was that my anguish had taken me beyond what people saw as appropriate.

I didn't do what most Christians do. I didn't compartmentalize my agony and say I was okay when I wasn't. I didn't go back to church to prove how strong I was so people could say, to my face, I looked good but get on the phone and talk about me. I didn't attend service, where I would become so over-whelmed with emotion people would have no choice but to come and care for me and give each other the "I told you so" look. Instead, I lived my misery out loud in those messy and chaotic ways. I told the truth about people who faked the funk during the week leading up to the funeral but disappeared as soon as we left the cemetery. I didn't mince words about tri-fling family members and the things they said and did to me. While I think folks understood my frustrations there, when I became loud about my frustrations with God, they really had a problem.

I hated God. I know we're not supposed to say that. I also know some people will either stop reading here or continue reading and believe there's no way I can be redeemed from what I just said. Others will use it as justification they knew I was reprobate all along. But it's the truth. When my mother died, I hated God. There was no way I could love God any-more. I was living my worst nightmare and God could have prevented it. There was no justification for taking her when God did and how God did. So, in my view, God didn't deserve my love and devotion because God hadn't given any love and devotion to us. My mother dedicated her life to God and I'm supposed to believe this was the best God could do concern-ing her? Nah.

And while I didn't need another reason to hate God, the three years following Mama's death provided more than enough. Going through a devastating breakup. Surviving sex-ual assault. Having a mental health hospitalization. Losing the fight to keep our home. Battling with my academic institution. Losing my dog, Langston, to kidney failure. It's as if hell-hounds were unleashed in my life. Honestly, it felt like God hated *me*. Like the feeling was mutual. Navigating that torture was already hard enough without hearing sermons about how good God had been in the past and how good God is right now. I didn't believe it and I wanted none of it. So I stayed home.

And if I'm even more honest, it wasn't just the sermons I didn't want to hear. I didn't want to hear from the people delivering them. Mama's death and subsequent events reopened old wounds and created new ones regarding preachers and pastors. Perhaps it started during the week of the funeral, when a pastor came by, offering condolences, and asked if I knew whether or not my mama had repented for being a single mother. Or it could have come flooding back when another one explained to me and my college suitemate that my mother's "new body" was going to be just like the one she had thirty-three years prior, before she gained the "baby weight." Janelle and I just sat there, both utterly amazed and insulted by his audacity. After he left, I told Janelle to tell anyone else who wanted to see me I was asleep. My friends passed around the message to insulate me from the foolishness. My mama was dead and two men came, in their official capacity as pastors, into her home to tell me either she was rotting in Hell for loving me or she was in Heaven getting back the Coke bottle figure she had before I ruined it.

As I grieved, pastors also entered my social media spaces

with unsolicited advice. A former pastor reached out to tell me young women were looking to me as a role model and I needed to think carefully about who I was encouraging them to become. "Because what you're going through is going to be over one day," he said. "But how you show them how to handle it will last a lifetime." I'd been raped a few weeks prior and not yet told anyone. When we got off the phone, I opened my laptop and deactivated my Facebook page. I stayed off the grid for three months.

The more comfortable I was becoming with how despair was "undoing" me, the more questions I had. The more questions, the more I resented the spaces and voices shaping women to think we couldn't be honest about how sad and painful things reorient us. I'd long abandoned the notion of being a "good, Christian girl" but, in this season of my life, I wanted to burn the façade to the ground. So many of us were suffocating and dying because we were trying to live up to a standard that isn't real. We were afraid to tell the truth—we knew we wanted to be free to live our lives as it felt honest to us—and I couldn't take it anymore.

I expected my then-pastor to understand that. Instead, she once told me I was leaning too heavily on our group chat. When I was hospitalized for suicidal ideation and severe depression, she told my friends she was on her way to the hospital, but she didn't come. And when I told her I was leaving the church, she dressed me down for unfairly attaching my grief to her church and, when referring to my new pastor, she called him a "good enough preacher."

What was true was, in the immediate aftermath of my

mother's death, I had been leaning on the group chat a lot. They were mostly older women; two of them were living without their mothers and I'd just lost mine. And while friends didn't tell me about my pastor's absence during my hospitalization until months later, I couldn't help but wonder if it was her way of getting me back because I hadn't been coming to church and returned a check the church had given me to assist with trying to keep my mother's home. And, even if I hadn't been attending services, I was in the hospital—fighting for my life. The least she could have done, when she told my friends she was on the way, was mean it. And the "good enough preacher"? He called while I was in the hospital, sent his ministerial colleague to visit me because he was away, and came to check on me when I was discharged. I was not yet a member of his church but he pastored me.

Truth be told, I was over preachers and I had good reason. Much of it had to do with social media. Whenever I spoke about sexism and patriarchal forces in the Black Church, Black male pastors had no problems coming for my neck. It was their way of publicly challenging and disciplining me. It didn't matter that I wasn't the *only* woman commenting on particular incidents, and it didn't matter that I wasn't the most prominent or degreed womanist or Black feminist speaking out, they came for me. And because I have no problems holding my own, I said what I said back. Many things can be said about me and some of them even will be true. But none of them will be more accurate than the fact that back then, if you came for me, I would do my best to ensure you wished you hadn't.

Much of what these pastors did amounted to severe gaslighting and proving they weren't doing all the progressive gender work they claimed. Their favorite rebuttal was that I speak in generalizations about Black men and Black male pastors and am dismissing the work they're doing in the church to dismantle sexism, homophobia, and all forms of marginalization. It would be funny if they weren't serious. And each time pastors tried to check me about my generalizations, they'd trot out their one or two personal examples of Black women who were able to excel in the church despite the sexism. They'd highlight the womanists or Black feminists they respected, who had no problem showing deference to them on social media and accepting invitations to preach their Women's Day services or be the lone female voice during their revival or pastoral anniversary celebrations. These women were used to show me that I didn't know what I was talking about or that they could say the same thing I said in a way that didn't make men feel uncomfortable. It didn't matter if these pastors hadn't read or critically engaged these womanists' works and it didn't even matter that their behavior fit squarely in the accurate descriptions of Black, cisgender, heterosexual male religious leadership these womanist works had been articulating for decades. I was seen as a problem and, for some reason, calling me out became a fun-loving sport. While it was enraging, it was also hilarious. If you closed your eyes, these men sounded just like the White men they spent so much time denouncing from their pulpits. Even more proof they wanted to be just like them.

Yet, as I remained frustrated that the face of Black Church

leadership was male and the vast majority of these men—
especially the ones with national profiles—weren't well read,
couldn't hold a candle to many of their Black women and
Black queer counterparts when it came to preaching and pas-
toring, and just weren't smart, I couldn't shake that the person
who was party to my greatest pain and shame was provided
insulation from accountability there. It did not help things
that the worst man I may ever know is a pastor. More treacherous than my father or my rapist—men who never tried to
be more than who they really are—he, like so many of his colleagues, was an emotional terrorist disguised as an emergency
responder. He knowingly destroyed the lives of those he loved
in secret, while preaching and teaching principles for holy,
ethical living.

Staying away from the church was the best thing for me.
Not only was my heart not there, but I needed time to mourn
the reality that losing my mother meant I lost church, too.
Therapy was essential in helping me articulate that the most
important aspect of church life for me was it being a space I
shared with my mother. I didn't have a memory about church
that didn't include her, and trying to create new memories
without her, while grieving her so deeply, wasn't the healthi-
est decision. The priority wasn't hearing another sermon. It
was trying to move through at least one day without becoming immobilized by tears. If I was looking for permission to
stay home from church, I'd received it.

Therapy also gave me room to work through my "stuff"
with preachers. It was layered. The pastor who sat my mother

down. The pastors who preached anti–single-mother sermons. The ones who insulted me and Mama in our home. The ones who attempted to silence me and my work. The one who told me I was too needy and didn't show up for me when I needed her. The one who broke my heart and those who let him and others get away with it. They made me wish Hell was real so they could rot in it. My therapist helped me to understand that while it may be vital to think through the institutional power of pastors and how my experiences manifested elements of their authority, lumping them all together and writing them off wasn't conducive to my own healing.

One of the greatest gifts womanist theology gave me was the validation of Black women's experiences. What we say happened to us matters. Full stop. It doesn't have to be qualified by anyone or mediated against another truth. It stands alone. Most of the pastors who called my work "generalizations" grounded in my own experiences attempted to negate that. They *weren't* just my experiences or my mother's experiences. Many Black women who spent any length of time in the Black Church were experiencing the same things. Sexism, patriarchy, and heteronormativity weren't innovative. They were trajectories of the harm Black women faced for attempting to love God and themselves. So much of this pain was part of our legacy.

But pain didn't have to be my inheritance. Piece by piece, my therapist helped me return to the pride I knew Mama had in being my mom. No pastor was able to shatter that then and she wouldn't want me to let them do it now. When I was dealing with the pain of a frayed relationship with the office of pastor, therapy gave me room to, first and foremost, lament. Like so many who grew up in my context, I had a deep reverence for the pastor. From childhood and throughout adulthood, the pastor was one of the most consistent men in my life. And the best pastors were the ones who knew to show care and interest to those of us whose fathers weren't in our lives. They didn't necessarily fill that gap for us but they wanted us to know they cared and were there.

Even as my thoughts about and relationship with the church has shifted, there are still some pastors I deeply love and respect. I am who I am today because they poured into me and still express a level of care and concern for my well-being. For this, I'm grateful. At the same time, pastors have been harmful to me. Too often, my experiences have been dismissed or I've been considered "strong enough" to take it. Some women possess a certain kind of self-assurance that prevents others from seeing them as victims. But I had been one of those women, and it was essential for me to express that I deserved more from people I held in high esteem and gave authority in a particular area of my life. Even if they didn't apologize, it mattered that I knew I was owed an apology.

Healing from specific encounters and walking fully in my healing were next steps. Admittedly, some were much easier than others. I don't ever have to see or speak to any of the pastors who insulted me or Mama again. I've limited my interactions to those with whom I share personal and professional circles. Some, I've blocked in my social media spaces. When it comes to telling why I don't deal with them, I tend not to share specifics. On some level, my actions spare them, and I recognize that's part of the problem. Pastors get away with a lot because we don't tell what they've done. But, more than saving them, I'm trying to save myself. You can tell your truth and everyone can know you're telling the truth. But a Black woman who details the pain she experienced at the hands of a pastor will always risk becoming a pariah. Sometimes, you do actually get to choose your battles.

Key to my healing has been remembering not all pastors are emotional terrorists. Some are actively trying to be different. I know because they're my friends and mentors. We have conversations about what it's meant for them to dismantle their privileges and work from a space that doesn't center their power and voice. I mean . . . my current pastor is a Black man trying to embody a different model of pastoral leadership, and I trust him with my life. He's one of the few Black men who can tell me about myself and I actually listen. He and others didn't deserve to be held hostage by the resentment and distrust in my heart. I owed it to them and to myself to let it go.

Working through my "stuff" allowed me to get to the heart of the matter. I was on a spiritual journey—one to make my faith my own. So much of who I knew God to be was rooted in my mother. I had to know God for myself and my knowledge would look different from hers. It was supposed to; my mother and I weren't supposed to have the same relationship with God. We aren't the same person. We were both created uniquely with our own idiosyncrasies. When it came to formulating my own relationship with the Divine, I don't know why I was so afraid.

More and more, I was becoming clear about my desired spiritual formation. I wasn't "just" Christian. Even as a child, I didn't believe Jesus was the only path to God. When we attended bible study, Mama would allow me to write questions and ask them only after she approved them. When she read some of them, she'd just look at me. "You would have some of the craziest stuff written down there and I wasn't about to have them folks talking about me," she'd say years later, when we'd laugh about it. But she was telling the truth. I wasn't fully sold on the notion of Christianity as God's preferred option and, if anybody knew that, they would certainly deem my mother unfit and consider my heresy a consequence of her pride and her unwed status.

I also wanted my faith to honor more of my Blackness. Christianity has African origins; this I know. I went to a Black church, but White folk allegedly shared the same faith and system of belief. That's why so many Black folk have something to say about the way White people choose to be Christian. I wanted to cut out the middleman. If there were Black people who were going to help White people be less racist and more like Jesus, then God bless them. But I wanted a spirituality known more exclusively to my ancestors and people who look like me.

And I needed it to be less male. I was tired of the heavy influence of men in my spiritual life. My pastor is a Black man— yes. But I was tired of hearing Black men talk about God.

Mainly, I was exhausted by the patriarchal presence within Black spaces because that presence wasn't just embodied by Black men. In the Black Church, some sisters could be as sexist as the brothers. The male influence was draining, as was the fact that despite them being statistically more religious than any other American demographic, Black women's voices and experiences were not at the forefront of any faith dialogue in the Black Church. I was tired of business as usual.

This fatigue cleared the way for me to explore for nearly two years away from consistent church attendance and membership. I joined a Buddhist community and attended their weekly gatherings. I studied African traditional religions and ways to listen for the voices of the ancestors, the orishas, and Spirit—seeking my true spiritual home. I read women's spiritual autobiographies, beginning with Sue Monk Kidd's *The Dance of the Dissident Daughter*. And what I learned is Spirit is everywhere, and the fluidity of the Divine only adds to its beauty. Equally, I was learning to trust the sound of the feminine in the spiritual space. If I trust Black women with all forms of my healing, then I trust them with my spirit. I couldn't go back to how things were before. Black women had hurt me and I'd hurt my fair share of sisters, too. But, ultimately, I knew who I could trust specifically with my well-being.

Slowly but surely, something was becoming apparent in ways I could no longer ignore. I was becoming less and less invested in the Black Church as my home base. That truth had come to me like a breath of fresh air, but it also scared the hell out of me. Who would I be without the church? Who *could* I be without the church and why, exactly, would I want to be that? These questions were weights growing heavier when I wondered what walking away meant, as well as the keys to unlock the last remaining chains holding me to an understanding of God and myself I had long outgrown.

To be fair, signs were pointing in this direction whether I wanted to admit it or not. I mean you've got to be pretty bold and over it to come late to church because you want to miss praise and worship but still find a way to sit no farther back than the eighth row. But it wasn't just that. I'd accepted the kind of freedom I was looking for, the kind of respect I desired as a Black woman, weren't going to be found in the Black Church. While many would consider my conclusion a bit defeatist, I recognized it was more real than anything else. For a woman who lives squarely at the intersection of faith and Black feminism, there are some concessions active church engagement requires, and I just couldn't make them. The church used to be home for me, but it wasn't anymore. Maybe I didn't need to be looking for *one* home anyway—rather, a community or village filled with all I needed to thrive. Maybe it was always too much to expect the church to be all I needed when so many robust spiritual experiences have gone into the making of me.

It took me a minute but I realized I didn't *hate* God. I was hurt and I think God understood me. And while I do not believe the suffering I endured was necessary to produce this result, I believe being open to how it could change me created conditions for this healing and growth. I am still unpacking all of what it means to finally admit I needed to part ways with the church as I have known it. Yet this new territory is a space filled with both fright and beauty, the wonder of the unknown and the fear of it without my safety net. Still, I have the testimony that walking away from the church brought me closer to God. And this closeness can see me through the fog of uncertainty as the next steps are made clear.

PSALM 90:12

One of Mama's favorite things to say to me was "I pray for your wisdom." Usually, it was her passive-aggressive way of telling me that whatever I was talking about was absolutely ridiculous and I was too smart to be so dumb. It would frustrate me to no end when she said this. I hated it, and whenever she did say it, a major fight ensued. Neither of us would really say "Sorry." Instead, she would send me money via PayPal. Or I would just come home and order food from our favorite hibachi spot. Apologizing to each other wasn't something we mastered before she left.

Not only would Mama say she prayed for my wisdom, she would bemoan that she no longer had my "ear"—her way of saying I wasn't listening to her anymore. In my defense, Mama just didn't get me anymore. Or so I thought. After she died, I would have given anything to hear her voice her frustration to me again. Mostly, I just wanted her to see my efforts to be wiser. I wanted her to know I heard her. Even when it seemed like I wasn't, I was always listening. And I hated that it took her passing for me to realize it myself.

Greater wisdom requires optimal spiritual health. As Minnie Ransom in Toni Cade Bambara's *The Salt Eaters* says, "Wholeness is no trifling matter." It goes beyond therapy and having a church home. We have to be connected to people who honor the totality of who we are, and we have to be willing to listen to them. I call these people in my life my "spiritual care squad." These six people have permission and access to hold me accountable spiritually and theologically. And while we may not share the same perspectives on everything, our relationships overflow with respect. The more I've turned to my spiritual care squad for guidance, the more I'm convinced every Black woman needs one.

Of the six, I've known Shayla the longest. We met after she moved to Winston-Salem and, ironically, we've been on similar spiritual journeys. At times, those paths intersected in ways surprising even us. Her journey led her to tarot card reading and Reiki training. Before any of that, she was my friend, helping me navigate the highs and lows of my life.

I met Bishop Laney while I was a student at Duke Divinity School. Aside from being one of the nicest men I'd ever met, he gave us preaching opportunities and genuinely cared about us beyond our professional abilities. When I moved to New Jersey and my life fell apart, he became more intentional about checking in. It meant more than I could ever articulate. I've never met a man I wished was my father more than Bishop Laney.

I met Reverends Anthony Bennett and Simeon Spencer,

both of whom I call by their last names, at the same time. Bennett and I were participants in the 2014 Black Theology and Leadership Institute at Princeton Theological Seminary. Spencer was a theologian-in-residence and our cohort leader. Immediately, we hit it off.

Two months after my mother died, I drove from New Jersey to Connecticut just to sit with Bennett and confess to him my frustration with God. I told him I'd not been praying. He told me something I'll never forget: "Every time you cry, you're saying a prayer." I held on to these words for dear life. I'd make the drive again to tell him I'd been sexually assaulted, and was embarrassed to tell him I had been dealing with a married man. Each time, he was as gracious as I'd always known him to be. He helped me see it wasn't him I needed to seek forgiveness from; I needed to find a way to forgive myself.

Spencer took me on as a daughter. Our relationship isn't just one of pastor-parishioner. With him I feel like family. For four years, I ate Thanksgiving dinner with his family. His wife, my soror, is my other mama. His children, my siblings. His siblings are my aunts and uncles; his nieces and nephews my adopted cousins. Every Sunday after church, I ate with him and his family and enjoyed his random texts of sheer foolishness to make me laugh. When I told him I'd been assaulted, he went into Papa Bear mode. For him it wasn't enough to know I understood that he was there; he wanted me to also know that he was going to be there if I chose to pursue legal action. When I joined Union Baptist Church in Trenton, he became my pastor for life.

I met Melva and K. Monet around the same time. *I think.*

You know how you've got those friends you have no idea how you met but can't see your life without them? That's Melva and K. Monet. Matter of fact, Melva, K. Monet, Shayla, and I have our own group chat where we check in with each other, share the occasional hilarious moment in our lives, and ask for prayers and accountability. Both Melva and K. Monet had a freedom in their spirituality as Baptist women I longed to know. I think they sensed it. As I grew more comfortable with asking them questions and seeking out their counsel, they grew comfortable providing wisdom and instruction outside the bounds of traditional Christianity.

There are many pastors, theologians, and faith practitioners I deeply admire. Their work has been impactful and key to shaping my own voice and forming my own faith. At the same time, they are not necessarily members of my spiritual care squad. Twenty years ago, my college buddy Jonathan told me, "Not everyone has permission to speak into your life." Just because people may admire us or find us significant, we don't have to give them intimate access, and no explanations have to be offered as to why, either.

Once when I was talking with someone about my spiritual care squad, they asked a rather frank question. "Why them?" On some level, I think they were trying to get at why they weren't on the squad but either didn't know how to ask it or didn't want to come out and say it. My answer was rather simple: "Because I trust them." None of them have ever made me feel like I was insufficient. They've not always agreed with something I said or a move I made, but they've never made me feel like I had to become something or someone else to be appropriate for God's love or whatever I desire.

They also are not fascinated by or enamored with me in any way. Be clear—they support me and want me to do my best. They've celebrated wins with me and have even shared where they can see me going. They've also listened and been wise counsel when I was trying to think through a decision. But they are not invested in my success as some extension of their own.

In addition, I trust their theological voices. I know they are working to create a more equitable and just world for all God's children. I know they are thinking through the difficult parts of our doctrine and working to make it more inclusive. I know God and the sacred community on the other side talk to them and they listen. And they talk back. So I can trust them. They make it easy for me to trust them.

But, above all else, I know my mother would approve of each of them. I marvel at how much I think like her. Some of us, as we get older, laugh at how much we become like our parents. For me, this is a real gift. If I don't think Mama would approve, I'm more hesitant about a decision. Mama had discernment. If she didn't feel it, she said as much and governed herself accordingly. And it was always revealed to be true. These are people my mother wouldn't side-eye and, should I ever add to the squad, the potential new members have to be folks who would receive Mama's seal of approval. She would have to be okay with them having my ear.

Some may call me elitist but there aren't people on my spiritual care squad who aren't qualified to be on it. We wouldn't go to a dentist who received training in law school; why would we seek spiritual oversight from people who aren't trained to provide it? Those on our spiritual care squad are there because they are knowledgeable, and we should honor their expertise. Social media gives every email address and password a platform, and we're in a moment when the instant you "check" the church, people will follow you. Those spaces are necessary, but they don't remove the need for training. My friend DeAnna says it best: "It's not enough for us to answer the call, we must also be faithful to it." And people who take their calls seriously, equip themselves. They go to seminary. They get certifications. And they have teachers and leaders who hold *them* accountable as they lead others.

I consider myself extremely churched and spiritually fluid. I am grounded by the teachings of Jesus, the wisdom of my ancestors, and the power of Black womanhood. If you can't honor my truth, you can't go on this journey with me. Those on my spiritual care squad respect it. And they're not trying to make me someone I'm not.

My spiritual care squad covers me when I'm going into an intense period of consecration and prayer. And I go to them for my beginning-of-the-year and birthday readings. They create prayers and rituals for me and help me process the existential questions life's experiences have brought my way. And there's room for them to speak whatever God and the ancestors have laid on their hearts concerning me. In this way, my spiritual care squad decentralizes power. So much of Black male power and the patriarchal structures in our com-

munity are rooted in the notion that only one can lead—
a messiah complex of sorts. The truth is many are equipped.
The messianic model, in many ways, disables accountability.
How can you challenge or correct someone when you're not
deemed their equal? A spiritual care squad shares responsibility and gives voice and authority to those who need it back.

The squad also reaffirms for me the interdependence God
originally desired for us. I believe creation was meant to work
together. The idea of domination rejects God's desire for collaboration. Spiritual care squads recognize we need each
other. We are a communal people. I don't intend to romanticize this in a way that negates the ever-present competitions
and tensions among us. At the same time, we are our stron-
gest together. Dustin always says, "Everything Zion needs is in
Zion." We are gifted to help each other.

Growing in wisdom, for me, wasn't just about having
healthy systems of accountability. It was also about understanding the mechanisms I needed to put in place to be healthier for myself and the people around me. I have a real problem
with boundaries, and I hate goodbyes. I partly blame this on
my mother's procreation partner. He should have been there,
he wasn't, and it shaped me in ways I was unwilling to admit.
And grief has a way of making a mess, too. Mama's death
upended me. My lack of boundaries after she died was simply for reasons of survival. My overall issues with boundaries,
though, spoke to a larger truth. I didn't really value myself. I
went into relationships trying to make them work. I started
them from the premise the dude wasn't going to stay. I didn't
see myself as valuable or worthy. If my father didn't stick

around, how could I be? How little I thought of myself played a direct role in what I allowed other people to do to me. There's an old adage that says you must teach people how to treat you. I don't necessarily know if I believe this, but I do think some of us have to teach ourselves how to treat us better.

Self-care has become commodified—a booming industry. But self-care isn't about what you buy or what you can do. It's about what you hold to be true about yourself. Once, I sat down to write a list of things I believed to be true about myself. For what felt like hours, I stared at a blank sheet of paper. I couldn't list my professional or academic accomplishments because even those felt hollow. (Impostor syndrome is a very real thing.) As I stared at that page, I wrote what I *wanted* to be true and to eventually believe. *I am beautiful. I am worthy of giving and receiving good love. I am enough, just as I am. I am already becoming who I need to be.*

Admittedly, I am still learning to accept these truths. But they have to be true to me because they *are* the truth about me. Self-care is honoring who I am. If I am good creation, then I am good creation. As Black women, we have to settle into more loving and freeing thoughts. So many books, conferences, podcasts, and sermons are rooted in the idea that we are not already good and must become good. That is not the truth of who we are. We are already good. There may be ways we don't lean into our goodness. Social and structural forces and our own fear can often dim the light of living into our goodness. Settling into yourself creates the opportunity to see yourself with grace and possibility.

When I realized I wasn't "broken Candice" anymore, everything changed. I have grown. I still have growing to do. But I could celebrate my growth. Too many of us love to proclaim we're not perfect. Saying so is quite unnecessary. We already know we're not perfect but continually repeating it only reinforces what we are "not" and doesn't uplift who we are. Realizing I am whole now has empowered me. I am able to chart my own emotional and spiritual growth. It required walking away from harmful theologies and, contrary to what people thought, I absolutely thrived when I did.

Coming home to ourselves makes some uncomfortable. The question my friend Teddy asked me when I bemoaned the painful transition of some friendships still gives me chills. "Have they ever seen you strong?"

Some people only know us broken. When I was making my way through years of sheer terror, some people saw a shell of me as my only identity. When I began to walk in my strength, it became a problem for them. It contradicted the narrative they had created about me. Some folks consider me to be mean on social media, particularly Facebook. While that's a space where Black Church respectability politics thrives, I don't subscribe to the notion of having to be "nice." If Black women aren't nice, then the world sees them as angry. I don't really care if folks see me as mean as much as I hope they understand my right to be who I choose to be.

But my grieving publicly, especially on Facebook, shaped how folks saw me. Some were introduced to me in that moment. As I regained confidence in myself and my voice, people didn't understand it and felt a way about it. We can't change how people choose to see us. What matters is who we are.

Those of us who have walked away from church and harmful ideologies may have found creating boundaries there the hardest task. In our culture, church is considered family. When we question theology, our loved ones take it as questioning them. They see it as passing judgment. They don't see our shifts as things we needed to do for ourselves. Rather, they take them as indictments of them and their faith. We want to yell, "This is not about you," but even that would be disrespectful. No matter how much we love these spaces, we can't go back. Despite false assumptions that we no longer love church or the people in it—including our families—we have to reject what is not true and embrace who we are.

There is power in saying no. Women don't say it enough and Black women say it even less. Saying yes to everything becomes "our reasonable service." American culture teaches men to say no almost without thinking, without a care about who it may harm or hurt. Women consider entirely too many people's feelings to the point of self-sacrifice and self-sabotage. "No" is a holy word. Our agency is sacred. God honors our agency through free will. We must honor it ourselves. When we say no, we are affirming that our capacities and intentions could be useful elsewhere. It doesn't mean we love the people asking us any less. Loving them actually has nothing to do with it. We should always love ourselves more. "No" is a complete sentence and offers no explanation. Because we care about the people we say no to, we choose to explain ourselves. But it's okay to say no and leave it there.

There will be people who reject our creation and enforcement of boundaries. Some people like unfettered access. Others like the power and moral superiority a lack of boundaries makes possible. People who bark at the boundaries you create have issues, too. But they don't realize we're doing them a favor. Even if they wouldn't say it, I drained my friends. Because they loved me and knew I was hurting, they allowed me to continually overstep. In doing so, I didn't respect their capacities to hold my stuff. It's painful to admit, but we have to be honest about the times we weren't healthy friends. I owe mine a depth of gratitude and an apology. Readjusting is hard but necessary.

When anything happens to me or around me these days, I have a simple prayer. *Lord, teach me to number my days.* I laugh at how quickly I rush to this scripture now, and I think about Mama. But, more than anything, it's exactly what I want to do. Since the next moment of life isn't guaranteed, I need reminders that I ought to live each moment with intention and care. Wisdom is defined as having knowledge and experience and making sound decisions rooted in said knowledge. I understand that more, now, than I ever did. When I look back over my life, particularly in the aftermath of my mother's passing, I want to take the knowledge gained from those experiences to be the best version of me for myself and others. That doesn't mean I will get it right. It means I'm trying, and that's the most I can ever do.

After a major test or presentation, whether I was in grade school or grad school, Mama would ask if I tried my best. When I told her I did, she said that was all she'd ever ask for and all I should ever require of myself. "Doing my best" means operating in wisdom, and it pains me that I can't tell my mother I understand now what she was trying to tell me. But I think she knows. I think she can see it. The ways I've tried and failed and succeeded. She's seen it all and she's proud. I'm finding my way.

CONCLUSION

Dear Mama,

Remember when I would sing Tupac's "Dear Mama" to you and you hated it? You would ask me, when was I ever hanging around with thugs and selling drugs, or what times I paid the rent when it was due, because you couldn't remember. As I sat down to write this, I couldn't help but laugh because I couldn't think of any other way to start this letter. I also couldn't imagine I'd be writing my first book without you here. You saw this. When you told me my calling was bigger than the four walls of the church and when you made me sit down and practice writing sentences and paragraphs, you saw this. You saw me.

And I can't think of a time when that was more true than when you wore red lipstick to my graduation from Duke Divinity School. So much was happening, I didn't even realize you were wearing it at the time. I remember you purchasing two tubes of Ruby Woo for the both of us a few weeks prior, and I saw it as the ultimate cosign. But, after you passed away and I got your cellphone, I saw the fierce red lip selfie session you took in the car before walking into Duke Chapel. Those pictures took my breath away.

If I'd known you'd be gone six months later, I would've made you take a picture with me when Maggie asked. We laughed as you gave me your signature smirk, said no, and walked away. Dustin did take a picture of the two of us later at the reception and has agonized, for years, over the fact that he can't find it. And while I would love to have those pictures, I've begun to realize those aren't the photographs I was supposed to have from that night. It was as if Spirit made you take those selfies in the car just for me.

Our theological disagreements were the stuff of legends. At the time, it felt like we were two people who didn't understand each other at all. For the life of me, I couldn't wrap my mind around how you'd push me to be inquisitive and a critical thinker in every area of my life but would, somehow, see it as disrespectful when I applied those same traits to concepts of faith and spirituality. And you would shake your head and tell me you raised me to be better than this. That my questions and my tone were offensive, not just to you but to the millions of Black women who saw Jesus as the way, the truth, and the life. When it came to these discussions, we often felt more like bitter rivals than conversation partners.

Often, I've wondered if those painful memories were the cost I had to pay for trying to be my own woman more than the daughter I *thought* you wanted. And even though I struggled with feeling worthy of being your daughter, you never made me feel like less than who you absolutely wanted. But I know when I disappointed you and I still struggle with that guilt. I wish I could make up for every single time I did something to hurt or disappoint you and it breaks me open over and over again that I can't. I know you'd want me to, as you would say, "let it go and keep it moving." I'm trying. It's hard.

Our conversations about being pregnant with me and how you felt you disappointed Grandma are exactly how I felt anytime you'd look at me with a twinge of disdain for something I did. I don't know if it's whether we want to be perfect in our mothers' eyes or we don't want yall to see particular flaws. I still remember the things about me that made you say, "Lord God today."

But who better to see and know my flaws than you? At every turn, you sought to nurture the hulled-out parts of me. "Who taught you to think like this about yourself, because I didn't" was a question you'd often ask when you became frustrated with my insecurities on display. And because I was afraid to tell you fully about how I'd learned much of it in church, I just let my Facebook statuses do the talking for me and assumed you'd put two and two together. I was terrified to tell you I thought raising me so tethered to the church was a mistake.

And how could I? I wasn't a single Black woman raising a child—a daughter, at that—at the height of the crack epidemic and gang violence. I wasn't dealing with a girl hitting puberty at the same time "superpredators" were roaming the streets of your community. I wasn't raising a little girl alone and wondering what I needed to do to ensure she didn't end up in the same situation years later. I didn't know what you were facing, and to come back and, as you would say, "be Monday morning's quarterback" would have been highly offensive.

But it wasn't your fault. You and so many mothers trusted the church. You were looking for safe spaces where we could grow and thrive. What better place than the church? You didn't expect I'd hear sermons demonizing you or that grown men would objectify and sexualize my budding body. You didn't know.

I watched you work tirelessly in congregations alongside people who thought they were better than you, simply because they were married. And some of these people forgot they weren't married when things first went down. You weren't the first person to be pregnant and unmarried in our family and, yet, relatives led me to believe you were. You weren't the first person to be pregnant and unmarried in our congregations and, yet, Christians led me to believe you were. You and the sisters like you deserved so much more. And something tells me you knew my generation would be the ones to call them on it.

You'd often get quiet when I'd say, "You raised me this way!" You knew it was true. Sometimes, you'd say you raised me to be *too* independent, which wasn't your fault, either. I had an amazing childhood, filled with adventure and wonder. As an adult, I think about how beautiful you made those years and have no idea how you were able to do it. I can barely take care of myself sometimes. By the time you were my age, you had a sixth grader. And while I'm grateful for your sacrifices, you weren't supposed to do this by yourself. Your procreation partner was supposed to help you and I hate that he didn't.

If I'm honest, having a mother like you and watching the ways you had to do this alone and hearing you become fodder for Christian gossip, there's no way I couldn't become who I am now. These experiences formed me. Call it me defending you—I know you wouldn't—but it just wasn't fair. Technically, the strength so many see in me is your fault. You told me there is power in one voice. You said it only takes one person to change conditions for others. You really harped on that. I bet you didn't think I'd take it to heart this way, huh?

You raised me in the church because you believed it was best for me. But church wasn't the only space of my formation. Hip-hop raised me, too. I still remember learning the words to Rob Base and DJ E-Z Rock's "It Takes Two" and performing it for you in our living room. Because I was seven, you saw that much differently than the time you caught me dancing and singing alone to Ginuwine's "Pony" when I was in high school. The brash "in your face" attitude of hip-hop was refreshing to me. It gave me permission to say what I felt and not let anybody run over me. Of course, it made for interesting conduct grades in school and seasons of punishment whenever report cards came out. These would be the times when you'd joke and say you found me in a cabbage patch because there was no way I could be your child. We were as different as night and day, sometimes.

But I think that's why you pushed me in the ways you did. You *knew* what would happen when I asked questions and sought the answers, didn't you? My thirst for knowledge didn't just stop with doing well in school.

I asked "why" a lot. Grandma still laughs about the time when I inquired as to why, if children's toys come from the North Pole, my bike said SEARS. Because the world was so filled with, as you would say, many unknowns to people who looked like us and we needed to level the playing field, I wanted to know everything I possibly could.

We really were robbed of more years of questions and an- swers. There was so much more I wanted to learn from you, and I'm sure there was much more you'd discover about me. My emerging faith and Black feminism were bringing so much to the forefront for both of us. I was becoming Candice in ways that, yes, made you uncomfortable at times but also were who you were raising me to be. The journey toward the answers was often cringeworthy for you but, now more than ever, I realize the journey had to be mine. It couldn't be about pleasing you, even if I wanted it to or thought it needed to be. It had to be about developing my own relationship with God.

We both know I was on this path long before you passed away, but losing you changed everything. I couldn't think of devoting my life to a God who took you from me. It wasn't fair, and while life itself isn't fair, God was going to get what- ever smoke I had for the Maker of Heaven and Earth. But, as I have fumbled in the dark to find my way, I'm understanding the beauty of my formation. It is a gift that you raised me to use my voice to raise concerns otherwise ignored. More and more, I realize you knew exactly what you were doing.

God really did make us all with love. Whenever you said this to me, it would sound trite. *God made us with love.* I knew God loves us, so whenever you said it, I would mumble under my breath. But this love God has for us is radical and transformative. It shaped a world full of possibility and promise. That hasn't changed; it's still there. Yet, it is what we project onto God's love and how we try to control it that causes the problems. You taught me that when we allow God's love to have free rein in our lives, we can fully live into the reality of God's intention for us.

"Red lip theology" has been my way of living into it—of reckoning with how racism, sexism, classism, and the politics of respectability left imprints on our faith communities and how those imprints have bruised our hearts and spirits. Red lip theology has been my attempt to return to the love with which God made us. I'm clear that the insecurity I carried because of my origins and because I thought I couldn't be worthy of love broke God's heart. I also know God was disappointed by some of my decisions, rooted in that lack of self. And I further know God holds the people and ideologies that harmed both of us accountable. They don't reflect God's heart and folks knew better. And we can be better.

Admittedly, I went to extremes in the infancy of my budding faith and feminism. I didn't know how to make sense of it so "throwing the baby out with the bathwater" was the only route I saw. Now I realize how this was the source of so much of your frustration. As I've gotten older and as I've had to adjust to life without you, I realize constructing and living faith is not as black and white as I made it seem. But I had to go to the extremes to find my way comfortably in the space where I believe I can best thrive and be who I believe God has called me to be.

My faith and that of sisters like me isn't necessarily going to look like yours. I wish more of our mothers understood this; it would ease so much tension. We're no different from you. We love God, we know God loves us, and we allow that love to guide our lives. I know I cannot survive without God in my life. It has been God holding my hand, in this darkness, enabling me to survive life without you.

At the same time, there are different ways God's love manifests itself in me—requiring I honor what I know to be true for me. It means I lean into religious expressions outside of Christianity; it means greater distance from the church than you would probably like. But it's authentic to the girl God led you to find in a cabbage patch one day.

When I set out to write this book, I didn't realize it would be about you more than anything. But why wouldn't it be? I am because you are. Your faith in God and in yourself and your belief in me made my life possible. I know God because of you, and it is the seeds of independence you planted inside of me and the search for knowledge you inspired that propelled me to come to know God, fully, for myself—saving my life and leading me to accept that life without you can still be beautiful and full of color.

Faith, as I now understand it, necessitates a certain kind of fearlessness. It doesn't mean we are not afraid. We're human; there are times when things will scare us. But the fearlessness faith calls forth is the kind that leads us to believe, if we get up and face the sun and put one foot in front of the other, those steps will eventually open up paths of healing and more life. And fearlessness requires we be honest about the things causing those steps to be harder than they need to be. It is the courage to name the ways the church and religious doctrine have been our stumbling blocks.

And no—my time in church wasn't *all* bad. I loved it. There is no other space where I was able to fully hone my voice and leadership skills in the way the church gave me room. It's for this reason I push back against it. I love the church and want it to be the best it can be. I need it to be better for the mother who, like you, believes the church is the safest place to raise her daughter. The church has to be what they both deserve. I'm giving to them what couldn't be given to us. May they receive it.

I will continue to cherish every photograph of you. It has been a joy looking at those pictures of you in your youth and seeing myself in your face. God has given me your laugh and your smile, and I am forever grateful. But it is the picture of you—with a flower in your hair and the smile that let me know everything would be okay—I will hold dear. Because, in it, we'd come full circle and didn't even know it. You'd bested the fears a twenty-six-year-old mother had of being good enough and worthy of God's love. You'd done what you set out to do: raise a girl who knew her worth and the power of her own voice. In finding yours, you gave me mine. Giving you the courage to slay in Ruby Woo was the least I could do. In this life and the next one, our love and bond are eternal. I am honored to be your love made flesh.

Candice

ACKNOWLEDGMENTS

God *loves* me. I didn't always believe that. I know it now. And I thank the Creator for the space and grace to come to know this truth.

I grew up hearing the committee chairs and presidents say, "If I start calling names, I'll forget somebody" at the end of every church anniversary and special service I've ever attended. I take that to heart here.

If I begin to name every single person who has been there for me throughout my life, I will surely omit someone by mistake. So, instead of naming you one by one, I would like to thank my family, friends, church members, choir members, classmates, professors, pastors, sorors, colleagues, and everyone else who has walked closely on this journey with me. Thank you to my group chats who are the real MVPs. Though I don't have to call each of you by name, you know who you are. And I love you.

To all my folks on social media, thank you for walking with me through the tough and crazy times to get to this very, very cool place. When I couldn't see the light, you became light for me. Thank you.

Specifically, I want to thank my grandmother, Helen Jackson Benbow. Thank you for taking me to all those usher board and missionary circle meetings. You're the first theologian I ever knew, and I'm more like you than we both initially realized. I love you so much.

Racquel Gill and Brandi Grove, thank you for saving my life when I wanted to end it. Had the two of you not loved me enough to get me the help I needed in that moment, I would not be here. Thank you is insufficient but I am grateful beyond words.

Of all the churches I have ever been fortunate enough to call home and hold close to my heart, I am truly grateful for Zion Hill Missionary Baptist Church. It will always be my first love and I miss it more than I can ever say. To the O.B. Cook and Messengers for Christ Choirs, thank you for being the family that Mama and I got to choose. Thank you for loving us both.

Rachelle Gardner, thank you for being more than an agent. Thank you for being an advocate, a champion, and a friend. You are so dear to me. Thank you for believing in me and breathing life back into me when I was ready to give up before I'd even gotten started. I can't wait to see all we do together!

Porscha Burke, I am clear that God brought us together. There aren't really words to describe the joy you've brought into my life, editing my words and becoming my friend. Thank you for taking my story and being kind and compassionate with your precision. Thank you for learning my voice and seeing my heart. I was serious when I told you that you aren't getting rid of me and I'm already thinking of what to put in the "first edit goodie basket" for the next book!

Tina Constable and everyone at Convergent and Penguin Random House, thank you for taking a chance on me and offering me a home. To everyone from copy editors to sales and marketing, thank you for all of your hard work. Together, I think we'll be able to do some really amazing things.

Melissa Harris-Perry, my Melissa, thank you for writing the foreword and being part of this. Most important, thank you for every word of encouragement down through the years. You have always been the blueprint.

Kennedi Carter, can you believe how far we've both come since that photo shoot at Monument of Faith? This moment is such a full circle. Thank you for saying yes and shooting my cover! I can't wait to see all the ways you will continue to change the world. I will never stop believing in your greatness and your heart.

There are many who started out with me on this journey and are now ancestors. They are a part of my great cloud of witnesses. I pray that I make them proud.

And there are some who aren't with me on this journey anymore, either because of something I did or something they've done. Whatever the case, I hope necessary apologies were made and accepted. I hope grace fills the space between us and that we've grown to be better people for ourselves and those still in our lives.

To everyone who will read this book, thank you for making one of my greatest dreams come true.

I am ... simply grateful.

ABOUT THE AUTHOR

CANDICE MARIE BENBOW is a theologian, essayist, columnist, baker, and educator whose work gives voice to Black women's shared experiences of faith, healing, and wholeness. Named by *Sojourners* as one of "10 Christian Women Shaping the Church in 2020," she has written for *Essence, Glamour, The Root, Vice,* Shondaland, *MadameNoire,* and the Me Too movement. Benbow created the #LemonadeSyllabus social media campaign, founded the media boutique Zion Hill Media Group, and, in memory of her mother, established the LouiseMarie Foundation to support HBCU nursing students and community mental health projects. A member of Alpha Kappa Alpha Sorority, Inc., Benbow holds degrees from Tennessee State University, North Carolina Central University, and Duke Divinity School.

www.candicebenbow.com
Twitter: @CandiceBenbow
Instagram: @CandiceBenbow

ABOUT THE TYPE

This book was set in Albertina, a typeface created by
Dutch calligrapher and designer Chris Brand (1921–
98). Brand's original drawings, based on calligraphic
principles, were modified considerably to conform
to the technological limitations of typesetting in the
early 1960s. The development of digital technology
later allowed Frank E. Blokland (b. 1959) of the Dutch
Type Library to restore the typeface to its creator's
original intentions.